ESCAPING FREEMASONRY

ESCAPING FREEMASONRY

A JOURNEY FROM DARKNESS TO LIGHT

JOHN F. MOSCATO

CONTENTS

Take no part in the unfruitful works of darkness, but instead expose them.

— EPHESIANS 5:11 (ESV)

FOREWORD
BY PASTOR STEVE GESUALDI

Stories of people "coming to Faith" are always a delight to my heart, and John's story is no exception. The occult is something that we have certainly heard of, and know exists, but rarely consider its reality and effects on people's lives, and on society as a whole.

John's experience and journey to freedom from the occult, and his transformation upon meeting Jesus, and coming to know him as Lord and Savior of his life, offers hope to people who may have been involved or impacted by the powers of darkness.

This book serves to make you aware of the subtle schemes and strategies of the enemy to ensnare people in vain philosophies and doctrines of devils. This book clearly shows that there is always hope no matter how entrenched they might be in the occult; and that they too, can make their journey out of darkness, and be part of God's marvelous kingdom of light.

You'll be blessed by John's experience and transformation. It's a timely work as many people are experimenting with the occult in search of answers.

Pastor Steve Gesualdi
Good News Chapel
Couture saint-Léonard, Qc, Canada

A PRAYER AND DECLARATION

Blessed are you, O Lord our God, King of the Universe who protects us and watches over us, who is good and who does good. You who abounds with love and compassion and are long-suffering.

Heavenly Father, I surrender my life to You. I renounce Freemasonry, the occult, New Age, and Satan. I cancel out any grounds or consents that I, any family members, or any of my ancestors have given to Satan that allow him to lay claims upon my life.

I further cancel all ancestral ceremonies, curses, rituals, sacrifices, blood pacts, or covenants that I, any of my family members, or any of my ancestors have contracted with Satan, especially concerning my family and me. I declare them all null and void in the name of Jesus Christ and place them all under the cleansing blood of the Lamb of God.

I declare of my own free will that Jesus Christ is my Lord and Savior. He died on the cross for our sins and was resurrected after three days. I declare my allegiance to Him and submit myself fully to the will of the Heavenly Father in all things, for my life and my home.

In Jesus' name, I pray, Amen.

INTRODUCTION

This is my attempt to explain the long and difficult process by which I came to the Lord. I've attempted to be as thorough as possible while explaining my bumpy road, shame, humiliation, and despair.

This is not to garner sympathy or pity but to show you that even if you've lived most of your life in sin, done or been part of things you're embarrassed and ashamed of, the Lord still has a plan for your life. No matter how badly you've screwed up or how deep you sink into despair, Jesus loves you, and if you give your heart to Him, He can and will turn your life around on a dime!

My story is a long and convoluted one; therefore, I've attempted to maintain a (mostly) linear chronology of events, avoiding rabbit trails whenever possible. I've never written anything this elaborate before, so your patience is greatly appreciated.

As children of God, we are rich beyond measure. If you've ever felt worthless and alone, like you weren't good enough or that your life wasn't necessary, know that Jesus willingly laid down His life so that you might be freed from the clutches of sin and death. He was willing to suffer a grueling, agonizing, and humiliating death at the hand of His persecutors. He was willing to give it all up—to save you.

My desire is to impart a sense of hope. From this testimony, the details of my suffering might spare you the tortured and difficult road I took. That it would help you avoid the pitfalls I fell into and that you might understand the unfailing love that our Lord Jesus Christ has for us all.

I also hope that if any of the people mentioned in this book ever come upon it, they'll see the error of their ways and repent. My goal is not necessarily to out the individuals but to expose the order's secrets.

CHAPTER I
HOW IT ALL STARTED

I grew up in a traditional Catholic family, but we were never particularly devout in our commitment to the Lord. Holidays were mainly family gatherings with gifts and food. There was little talk of the significance of these holidays beyond the superficial explanation.

In grade school, we had catechism classes, so I knew who Jesus was, at least intellectually, and understood the overall story of the New Testament. But at such a young age, it held no significance for me. The tragedy in this is that the Bible is, without question, *the most* fascinating book I've ever read. However, you'd never know it from the dull, monotone way the nuns who taught us conveyed it.

They ignored most of the supernatural elements in the New Testament, and The Old Testament was all but rendered nonexistent. Our only meaningful contact with the Old Testament was when we watched part of "The Ten Commandments[1]" on an old tube T.V. set that was wheeled in from the audio-visual department, and that happened just once in grade school at Easter. As far as I was concerned, it was just a fairytale for grown-ups shared with children, something revered but never lived or put into practice.

They usually enforced church attendance with threats or violence. The fruit of the Spirit? Kindness, patience, gentleness? Seemingly, these were the elements of fairytales. My parents weren't what you'd call understanding, compassionate types. From my earliest memories, they typically met the slightest challenge to their authority with violence.

When raised by people who are habitually violent, abusive, and have difficulty controlling their tempers, childhood is spent in constant fear for safety. You can't help thinking that God, whoever or whatever He is, either has a cruel sense of humor or doesn't exist.

The arguments put forth by atheists against the existence of God weren't what drove me away from Christ. It was mostly my family's questionable and sometimes shameful behavior.

My parents expressed reverence for the saints; they regularly attended church and were polite and kind to the people we met there. But as soon as we got home, it all evaporated. What was a 7-year-old boy supposed to take away from those dreary, 45-minute sermons by a monotone priest who seemed about as excited to be there as I was? None of those sermons ever translated into meaningful or concrete actions throughout the rest of the week.

Church never equipped my parents to handle meaningful questions about God, life, or divergent opinions, despite being lifelong Catholics. Anything that challenged their beliefs, preferences, pride, or perceived authority met with threats, bullying, denial, or rejection. And while a certain softness creeps in with age, the approach to dissenting ideas and challenging concepts remains unchanged.

My parents seemed more concerned with being well-perceived by society than they were with upholding fundamental values. The actual well-being of the family, or their children, was a secondary consideration. This led to me being an unusually angry and unhappy child.

Whenever I'd come home from school, I felt dread. I couldn't understand how other kids could go home from school eager to see their parents. Sometimes my parents were nice, and I genuinely think they wanted to be good. Then something would happen, they'd get a phone call, I'd make some back-handed comment, or something would happen at work. Anything at all that brought my father displeasure caused him to turn on a dime.

Then came the violence. To see how quickly my father could become enraged was a terrifying sight to behold; you never knew what might set him off. I was often terrified because I thought he had lost control of himself and there was no telling what damage he would do, almost as though someone flipped a switch in him. He might have felt remorse afterward, but the damage was already done.

No one saw the dysfunction within my family. Or no one thought enough to do anything about it. Not schoolteachers, social workers, police officers, priests, doctors, or neighbors. No one. Every institution created to protect people and defend justice and fair treatment within society had utterly failed my family and me. I suspect my family was desperate to cover up their dysfunction, and other people didn't want to acknowledge the abuse in my family because they were likely guilty of similar things themselves.

No one wants to be the bad guy, the guilty one, the object of rebuke, but what's the alternative? It's one thing to grow up in a faithless household without sound foundations to build on. What about those who have been raised in the faith their whole lives? Do they have a duty to ensure that the values they're passing down and espousing are in harmony with God's Word? I believe God is always talking to us, inspiring us, and urging us to take the path of righteousness, regardless of whether we believe in Him.

God works with our flaws because He loves us, but we must also be willing to do our part. That means heeding His Word and being obedient. God doesn't need us, but He delights in His children being active participants in His Kingdom.

Some people, however, are adept at drowning out the voice of the Holy Spirit. Some people love indulging their sinful nature with drugs, alcohol, rage, lust, greed, laziness, willful ignorance, pride, etc. For those people, the Holy Ghost's words become the scathing indictment they desperately flee from, and you can do that if you choose. But it comes at a price.

There comes a time when—like at the Tower of Babel—we willingly choose to deny the Lord and turn our face from Him. God never forces His way into our lives: He knocks politely, and if we don't desire His presence, He honors our choice. He may grant our desire and turn us over to the false gods we love so much. Another example of this is Saul, the first King of Israel. Not only was Saul chosen by God as King, he also received the gift of prophecy. He had it all; he carried a divine anointing and won battles against Israel's enemies. But because he became proud and willingly chose disobedience, God's Spirit departed from him.

That can happen with individual people, but it also happens to churches. Is it any wonder that some congregations have seen their attendance dwindle to nothing in the last 35 years?

Christian values, to some, are like the statues of the Saints: wooden and just for show. The term "white-washed tombs" comes to mind, and it's no surprise that God has removed the lampstands from such churches. In my estimation, the Catholic Church and hypocritical Christians have done more to drive people *away* from Christ than atheists ever could. Most non-believers accept my faith, even if they don't share it.

You'd think people who claim to love the Lord would read His Word and try to understand it. But most Christians spend less than an hour a week studying or reading their Bible. I don't recall ever seeing my parents read it, and aside from when my father went to a few short-lived Bible-study classes, he never cited or referred to The Bible. He'd refer to the Catholic Saints, but that was usually in trying to justify something questionable he'd done. I've forgiven him and my whole family, though the issues remain.

We need to read His Word regularly to remember. When we forget, seemingly benign but dangerous ideas can creep into our minds. When we hear those dangerous ideas repeated regularly, we normalize them. Like a newly crowned tooth, it feels familiar after a while, to where we even forget that it's not natural.

The Devil doesn't have to send you radically off-course, just a couple of degrees here and there. Before you know it, you're headed in a completely different direction than what Scripture prescribes, and you're oblivious to it.

Worse yet, people recoil when someone comes along and politely points out the glaring error in that defective doctrine. Dissent is silenced, and its authors ostracized. People have lost the ability to debate; perhaps they never had it. Maybe that's why so many quickly shut down any discussion and resort to censoring those who say things they don't like.

Now don't get me wrong, expulsion and ex-communication can be useful and occasionally necessary when scripturally supported: we're expected to confront people on their errant behaviors, especially when dealing with repeated, unrepentant sin, but we ought always to remember that we're flawed beings too, and we might be the one in the wrong. I wish there were an attempt at such a debate and exploration in my congregation those many moons ago. Every single one of us has fallen short of the glory of God. Every. Single. One!

Perhaps if we'd put ourselves in our neighbor's shoes occasionally, it might incline us to tread a little more gingerly.

Throughout my teens and twenties, I identified as an atheist. Good and evil were just perspectives, not absolutes. I only admitted fault when caught and cornered, and whatever was needed to succeed in life was acceptable. Alas, for me, the damage was done. I believed that when I died, my remains would decompose into fertilizer, and that was the end of me. What a terrible and shameful way to live.

Yet, even in the darkness, God used me in ways I wouldn't understand until many years, even decades later.

CHAPTER 2
SOMETHING LIKE A PHENOMENON

At an early age, I showed artistic talent that surprised my parents, peers, and adults. I started drawing as soon as I could hold a pen or pencil. I honed this talent over the years, and when I reached college age, I was ready to study and perfect my skills as an illustrator.

As part of our curriculum, our teachers gave us various illustration projects to let our creativity shine. One of those projects, circa 1992, involved the creation of a corporate logo for a fictitious advertising campaign or poster. The design I rendered, which I've kept all these years, features a double "A" shaped similarly to the Freemasons' square and compasses. I had no clue what a Freemason was or what their logo looked like.

Approximately a year later, another similar project was a fictitious ad for Camel cigarettes. Like the previous one, the illustration I produced was eerily prophetic for me: I rendered the brand's mascot, Joe Camel, dressed in a black suit with a white shirt, standing on a black-and-white checkerboard floor. Once again, unbeknownst to me, I'd created unmistakable symbols used in Freemasonry.

I completely understand if you think these don't seem like particularly "positive signs" because they all point to the occult. I still don't think that these symbols or associations were designed for me to understand. With nearly a quarter century of hindsight, I've realized that God was planting seeds. He showed me glimpses of the future, leaving breadcrumbs He knew I would decipher when the time was right.

In 2003, about a decade later, I met and began dating a young woman from Argentina. Again, two more interesting breadcrumbs dropped. For one, this woman had a propensity for dressing in black and white, calling back to the attire of the occult orders. The second came when she introduced me to her country's national beverage: yerba mate, a most foul-tasting tea (my sincere apologies to any Argentineans). She found the brand she was familiar with back home. When she produced the packaging, it etched the image into my mind. On the main panel was a large, red Maltese Cross; a symbol used by occult orders, such as Freemasonry and the Knights Templar.

In hindsight, the tea's bitter taste foreshadowed things to come, but we'll get to that later.

I became interested in the New Age movement. In years past, I had occasionally experienced sleep paralysis and night terrors. I had heard and read of people having out-of-body experiences. While many of those testimonies could be explained away, many could not. Some were so baffling that they compelled me to consider the possibility that there was more to life than what we could see, hear, feel, taste, and touch.

At this point, Christ was the farthest thing from my mind. Still, I was very much on His mind. Besides the breadcrumbs He left previously, He also used the New Age movement like a rudder to guide me back onto the narrow path that leads directly to Him.

There's something about God that isn't blatantly spelled out in Scripture: He is the undefeated and undefeatable Master of improvisation! However catastrophically you think you've messed up your life, He can turn it around on a dime. Don't believe me? Read on…

In my mid-thirties, my sister Suzanne loaned me a book titled *Buddha's Brain: The Practical Neuroscience of Happiness, Love, and Wisdom.* While I had casually flirted with New Age concepts, it had been more like amusement up to that point. Now I was reading about how meditation and specific visualization exercises could "re-wire" my brain and increase happiness and peace—or so I thought. This led to things like yoga, mandalas, healing crystals, and similar talismans, which I'd begun accumulating.

Near this time, I started having strange, cryptic, vivid dreams. One such recurring dream involved finding opened doors to my house as though someone had been in my home and left without me even knowing.

I clearly remember one dream after all these years that happened at my parents' house. I felt a mysterious pull towards the front door as if the doorbell had been rung. When I opened it, a woman stood there, mainly wearing dark clothing. At first, she seemed normal looking, then she suddenly assumed an aggressive stance, as though she was about to run me over to enter the house. In a panic, I shut the door on her and woke up!

A similar woman appeared in a dream at least once more. I dreamed I was walking to the bathroom at my house this time, and this woman was already standing in the corner of my bathroom! Then I woke up.

As if the dreams weren't enough, I began seeing things I'd never seen before. Specks of light would appear out of the corner of my vision, almost as if a large piece of dust floating through the air might catch the light at just the right angle and get your attention. When I'd turn to look, it was no longer there. I initially dismissed the phenomenon as purely secular—the sun's reflection off a watch crystal shining on the wall or dust.

The problem was that the latter could be reproduced by turning your eyes back to where you were looking to catch that piece of dust or purposely shifting your watch to catch the sun again. However, these specks of light were different, and many times they occurred in places where there was no natural light and nothing to reflect from. Much to my surprise, these specs of light didn't seem brighter in dark places. They were always just noticeable enough to get your attention and then disappear as soon as you turned to look right at them.

I experienced no dread at the specs of light but rather curiosity. It would be years before I connected these with other bizarre phenomena. For instance:

- Part of my job during this period involved casting polyurethane resin parts for model kits, which I did from home, and sometimes, I would leave them on a countertop to harden fully. One time, I went to check on some parts that had come out of a mold in perfect shape, and it surprised me to find that one part had become utterly deformed. It was as though someone had inserted a straw into a piece of Jell-O and blew air into it until it exploded from within. This phenomenon only occurred once; I could never reproduce this effect, despite using the same batch of resin many times.

- The television in my home was in the corner of the living room, and a VCR was atop it. Occasionally, the VCR would turn itself on, make sounds like it was loading a tape, and promptly turn itself off again. This was despite the remote not being near me and often having no batteries.

- At night, while lying in bed, I could barely hear what seemed like a muffled conversation, as though a television was turned on in another room, but nothing was on.

- The apartment where I lived in made odd cracking and popping sounds, as though someone was walking across an old wooden floor, but these sounds emanated from the walls and ceiling. These noises even startled some guests on occasion.

- I started having erotic dreams which were unusually vivid.

- I occasionally experienced a phenomenon commonly known as sleep paralysis. I would wake up in the middle of the night and find myself unable to move or even speak while being completely alert.

- On one particular occasion, I was in bed around 5 a.m. I was in that state between sleep and awake when I noticed a shadowy figure entering my bedroom (back when I used to sleep with the door open). This figure approached me, and while it had no distinct shape, it "felt" like my grandmother. It put one "hand" on my right shoulder and the other on my thigh. I reached out to touch it, and it was gone!

Besides these phenomena, I started having more shivers than I ever had before, like the ones you get when watching a really scary movie by yourself. I've experienced these since childhood and initially wrote them off as just a natural feeling of fear that people sometimes experience. But these had come with another, more unpleasant feeling, as though I was being watched.

While all the phenomena listed above would have surely been a massive red flag to anyone with a Biblical mindset, I hadn't connected those dots yet. Further, these events were spaced out over several years. Because I hadn't experienced anything outright harmful (yet), I chalked most of them up to various spirits merely wanting to contact me or get my attention. I was intrigued by them and had not yet connected the paranormal activity to demons. While I now believe that things like yoga and meditation kicked things into a high gear, my family had also experienced similar phenomena, all the way back into my childhood and possibly earlier.

CHAPTER 3
PARANORMAL ACTIVITY

While these manifestations took place over 4 or 5 years, in 2008, I was determined to get some answers. While awareness of the Bible existed in the back of my mind, I had convinced myself that the answers would be more readily found in Eastern/Buddhist/Shamanic sources. I thought all religions had an aspect of truth, but we needed to take those bits of truth from here and there and put them together for ourselves.

In Western culture, we commonly think the grass is greener on the other side of the fence—the other guy or religion has the answers. I thought truth and immortality had to be earned.

However foolish and deceived you may have been in your life, know that there was someone like me who was more foolish and more deceived than you were.

My quest for truth led me to explore many exercises and disciplines, including Shamanism.

My sister Suzanne had been steeped in New Age for many years. She introduced me to Christopher, a shaman she was acquainted with. He invited me to a personal meditation ceremony called a Shamanic Journey. The process was relatively simple: after being "purified" with sage smoke, he began rhythmic drumming, and in my relaxed state, I "journeyed" into the spirit realm. There, the spirits showed me what I needed to see.

My vision was of coming out of the ocean and walking into a large forest clearing. In that clearing were many types of bizarre creatures. Some looked vaguely human, and others like giant eels floating through the air and snaking between lush, green conifers. It's almost like they were trying to convey that these creatures were my extended, spiritual "family."

I looked beyond the forest toward a dry, desolate Grand Canyon-like landscape. In the background, I saw a nuclear explosion and what looked like a Native American man standing next to me, glaring at me as if to say, "Why did you do that?" Then, I was brought into a quieter, rocky place below ground. The cave sloped downward, and I saw what looked like a fountain near the bottom. There was no water in it, but yellow-green pus oozed up from the ground beneath the fountain.

Though I didn't realize it then, I now believe God used this vision to reveal the severe decay deep down within me, something I needed to address. A dream I had some time later corroborated this: I was in a car, driving under an overpass chiseled directly out of the mountainous landscape. I saw the part of the mountain chiseled away for the underpass looked like a badly decayed tooth. As if to say that the structure beneath the surface, the foundation of the work, was rotten.

I cringe when recalling those dreams, but I'm also moved by how patient and dedicated God is with all of us. He knows that confronting our decay is sometimes a long, painful process, so He feeds us more digestible, bite-sized morsels.

Regardless of what it took, I wanted to learn the truth. I was determined to understand these dreams and learn why my family and society were so dysfunctional. I never uttered it verbally, but in my head, I recall thinking to myself, *God, please help me find the Truth, no matter the cost.*

I didn't think God was listening, but He was. He sees into our hearts, He knows our every motivation better than we know ourselves, and He loves us even when we reject and deny Him and His goodness. God answered my prayer, but rather than just spoon-feed me some facts that I'd likely dismiss and reject, He took me on a journey. One that allowed me to gain understanding and connect the dots myself.

He helped me build a case for His glory by allowing me to wallow in the filth of my idolatry and see what life without Him looked like. He was going to let me experience what the adversary offered. He loved me enough to not shelter me from the pain and suffering of my own bad choices. He loved me enough to let me choose. Is it not written that He punishes and corrects all those he loves?

God had a plan.

Unbeknownst to me, this recent excursion into shamanism led me to something far more sinister. In the fall of 2008, they invited me to take part in a 2-day shamanic workshop held at the local Masonic Temple on Sherbrooke Street in Montreal. While I had traveled down the conspiracy rabbit hole two years prior and learned some unsettling information about the Masons and their practices, I was still determined to take part in the workshop.

I voiced my reticence to hold the workshop in the Masonic Temple, but the organizer assured me they were fine, upstanding people. You'd certainly get that impression from the outside.

Many Masons and Shriners are involved in charity and philanthropic work in their respective communities, so I had difficulty harmonizing my findings with their public image. I played the wait-and-see card until additional facts were brought to my attention.

Not long after this event, my dreams took an eerie turn. In one dream, I was walking home, and upon entering the apartment, I heard the water running in the kitchen. I discovered the tap was running into a clogged sink.

Then I found myself right outside my bedroom, standing before what seemed like an impossibly tall Native-American man with long, wavy, salt-&-pepper hair and a faded black jean jacket and pants. While we spoke no words between us, he looked down at me with a neutral expression I couldn't quite understand. It was as though he wanted me to know that he was my "spirit guide." Demons are spirits, too, who can guide you, but you probably won't like the destination. While I was unclear about the meaning of this dream, the next one would be hard to miss—or so you'd think.

January 2009, in my dream, I was holding a small antique music box. It felt like a family heirloom, made of ornate brass, and had a red felt lining. I noticed a small piece of ash inside when I opened the lid. I felt some sort of demon spring forth from the ash and enter me. I began to howl and roar like a wild animal! I woke up screaming and terrified, with my heart racing.

Although unpleasant, I believe God had just revealed a critical puzzle piece in understanding what I was involved in. While I had engaged in behaviors and activities that allowed demons to come in, I had also inherited evil spirits from my family. They were slowly but surely driving me to the edge of the precipice. While I may be in the minority in my thinking, I don't believe evil spirits always want to kill you; many times, their goal is simply to create as much chaos and suffering within a group or family as possible, explaining why there are quiet periods interrupted by intensely stressful situations.

Looking back, I recall several instances of demonic presence or influence. I experienced frequent night terrors as a child. I also had a lot of trouble with pets suddenly behaving aggressively, especially around my father. I've lost count of all the times I've seen dogs (and even a rabbit) growl and bark at him or try to bite him. Birds would swoop in and dive-bomb him as he was gardening. Even domesticated birds and rabbits became unusually agitated in his presence.

There was one instance when my father bought me a pet goldfish, which I kept in a small bowl downstairs on the countertop. One morning, my father came downstairs and claimed he found the fish half-dead on the floor, at least 2 feet away from its bowl. It's as though something either scared the daylights out of the fish, causing it to jump out of its bowl, or something removed it from its watery abode.

I also remember hearing of odd things happening to some tenants in my dad's building. One incident involved a family of four who rented one upstairs apartment. Their youngest son came onto the back balcony and began throwing kitchen knives down on the people below. Years later, another tenant confided to me he sometimes felt like someone (or something) pulled the blanket off him as he was sleeping.

Perhaps the most significant and unmistakable of these paranormal events happened to my sister Suzanne in the mid-eighties; I wasn't present and only learned of this event years later. She lived with a roommate, and they weren't on good terms. One day, alone in her apartment, Suzanne encountered the appearance of a tall, thin man.

Her roommate ridiculed Suzanne when she tried to tell her about the apparition. Sometime later, her roommate also witnessed the apparition, much to her surprise and horror.

When Suzanne mentioned the apparition to our mother, she received a chilling response: our mother told her she had been praying to our deceased "grandfather" to chase my sister away! Clearly, not the mark of a loving mother and a happy, well-adjusted family.

CHAPTER 4
A MYSTERIOUS ORGANIZATION

The following year and a half was relatively uneventful. Paranormal activity continued, but there was neither an increase nor a decrease. I met some people in so-called "conspiracy circles" and stumbled upon some interesting information on occult practices. The sources were dubious, so I didn't give much credence to them. I wasn't sure what to make of the people themselves, but that was all about to change.

In the fall of 2010, a friend and I attended a book fair. One of my newfound acquaintances, Sylvain, was premiering the launch of his new book on the inner workings of the credit system. While the fair itself was not memorable, the conversation we had afterward certainly was. One thing led to another, and we talked about the inner earth, lost civilizations, and the connections to the occult.

The way Sylvain spoke about the subject caused me to think he was holding back, as if he knew more than he was letting on. I remember saying, "All this is fascinating; I'd really like to know more." When I said that, Sylvain froze as if I'd unwittingly uttered a mysterious password.

Sylvain paused, then pulled a small piece of paper from his jacket and wrote a single name and phone number on it. He said, "Call Maryse, tell her you know me, and you'd like the time and address for the next conference."

Conference? What? What was going on? My other friend seemed uninterested in what had just happened. You might even say he was oblivious to it. He soon decided that it was getting late, and he needed to leave. After he and I said our goodbyes, Sylvain and I chatted a little more. He explained he was part of an organization and that, besides its regular (and undisclosed) business, also organized private, spiritual conferences that would answer some of my questions. He suggested I bring something with which to take notes.

To say that he was being deliberately cryptic is an understatement. I pressed him on the name and nature of this mysterious organization, but he merely told me that my answers would come in time. I was intrigued, but I slept on it instead of calling.

My curiosity eventually got the better of me, so I called Maryse, and she provided the requisite details for the conference, which was in a few days. It was an out-of-the-way place in Longueuil, not too far from the metro station and not a good part of town. The unlocked door of the address opened to a flight of stairs upward to a small, unremarkable banquet hall.

Two ladies greeted me at the door, one of whom turned out to be Maryse. She asked who I was, so I told her my name. She remembered me from the conversation we'd had several days earlier. She was friendly but guarded, as though she was trying to figure me out. The whole thing was odd, but not enough to set off any alarm bells in my head. Not yet at least. Maryse asked me to sign a registry and suggested a donation of twenty dollars for the conference. Fair enough, I thought.

After finding a chair in the room of maybe 60 people, I noticed that the lead conferencier, a rather average-looking man in his early fifties, was conversing with one guest. I couldn't help but notice the little gold pin on his jacket: a double-headed eagle. He rang a small brass bell to call the group to order and begin the conference.

The month's topic was mantras and how to use select verbalizations to activate healing and perform specific tasks. It was my first time having experienced such a detailed presentation on an occult subject. Taking notes was recommended and I immediately understood why. They even encouraged us to practice these newfound mantras at home as an assignment.

I noticed Maryse sitting in a chair, somewhat removed and far behind all the other guests, almost as if she were studying us. While that was certainly strange, the conference itself was so interesting that I didn't give it much thought. Near the end, the speaker produced a bag of trinkets he said had come from his last trip to Nepal and distributed them selectively.

He motioned to me and addressed me as if he knew me. He handed me a small brass medallion with a red and black cord that he said he was "instructed" to give me.

I was a stranger there and immediately made to feel welcome; what a great group of people, I thought. Had I known then what I know now about that man and the organization he was a part of, I would have run out of there, leaving a me-shaped hole in the wall—door be damned! But I was so overwhelmed with fascination and curiosity that I happily accepted the gift.

The next conference was in a month. Little did I know that human and inhuman on-lookers were carefully scrutinizing me.

A few days passed, and I contacted a mutual friend of Sylvain and me on Messenger. Franco was an acquaintance I'd met through another friend, and he shared my interest in esoteric subjects. I told him I'd attended a spiritual conference Sylvain recommended. To my surprise, Franco had previously attended a few as well and had nothing but praise for them.

I remember telling Franco how I thought Sylvain was such a mysterious character. Then Franco dropped the bomb on me, saying, "You know he's a Templar Knight, right?" I could feel the gears in my head engage violently as I struggled to understand what he'd just told me. I had read some material on the Knights Templar and how they were wicked occultists who used Christianity to cover their nefarious deeds. Yet, Sylvain seemed like a nice guy, generous and helpful. I was decidedly wary, but simultaneously curious. I advanced cautiously to see if I could find out the facts for myself.

The conference I'd attended had been informative and helpful, nothing like the malevolent people I had read about. Franco reassured me and said that he'd be attending the next conference. He also told me he was taking another course offered by Sylvain on operative magic. He'd be bringing a friend who was also taking that course to the conference. With my concerns assuaged, I was determined to be at the next rendezvous.

The December conference was a different topic, but was just as fascinating and followed the same general pattern as the previous one. When it was over, the speaker (who I later knew as Denis) asked to speak with me, Franco, Franco's friend, and Sylvain, who had also attended. We stood outside in the snow while Denis inhaled his cigarette. He received a call and spoke apologetically to his mysterious caller, as though he was trying to smooth over some kind of dispute. He ended the call and mumbled about some sort of misunderstanding with the Dalai Lama's secretary.

Wait, what?

Apparently, I was to believe that some guy I've never heard of, who gives conferences in a run-down suburb of Montreal, was on speaking terms with the Dalai Lama. I wasn't buying it, but I humored him.

He started speaking to me about my life and all the suffering I'd experienced and how things were about to change for me. Reaching under his shirt collar, he pulled up a gold chain, upon which was some sort of amber pendant. He told me that the pendant had been a gift from the Dalai Lama, and he wanted me to have it. He unclasped the pendant and handed it to me. Not wanting to be rude, I accepted the gift with a mixture of puzzlement and thankfulness. Franco and his friend both seemed surprised by the gesture and asked to see the pendant, in awe of this little trinket, as if I'd been handed a piece of the true cross!

Sylvain observed silently, his grin readily evident. Before we parted, Denis told me I was ready, and it was time for me to "graduate" to the big boys' school. Dumbfounded, I didn't ask what that meant. I let the events settle in my mind and tried to make sense of it all after I had a bit of distance.

Some guy I'd only met twice tells me about my life, hands me a trinket that allegedly comes from the Dalai Lama, and tells me it's time to graduate to something higher; what could be wrong with that?

CHAPTER 5
THE GRAND LODGE

Sylvain remained characteristically evasive regarding this "big boys' school" and seemed to enjoy that I had no clue what was happening. At the closing of the January conference—a packed house—Maryse called Franco and me aside and handed each of us a plain brown envelope in Sylvain's presence. She told us it was an application form for their organization, which Denis mentioned to us just last month.

"What organization is it?" I asked.

Sylvain answered, "Freemasonry," while beaming a magnificent grin.

"Aren't you a Templar Knight?" I asked innocently.

I noticed Maryse flash a displeased look towards Sylvain, who, being quick on his feet, said that we should start by reading a book called *Freemasons for Dummies* and it would all make sense. He also organized a meeting with us so that he could answer questions we had about the order. Then, we could start filling out our application forms if we wanted to proceed with our membership.

Well, that was awkward!

As bizarre as all this was, it was also exciting. I really couldn't help feeling like a little boy who had been taken aside, made to feel like he had a calling, and given a magical ticket to some mysterious Neverland that "normies" didn't have access to.

The entire experience, I later deduced, was intentionally designed to make the neophyte feel special and privileged; that's how cults work. The drug dealer that gives you free samples isn't doing so out of the goodness of his heart or because he's your friend. He wants something from you, something you wouldn't give to him if you knew his true motives.

The required reading of *Freemasons for Dummies* left me with more questions than answers. When the informal "orientation" with Sylvain came, I asked a few questions.

I was told that most of what circulated about Freemasons was disinformation borne out of ignorance, jealousy, envy and/or fear. I was told they persecuted Masons throughout history, which was part of why they were so secretive. It was also said that the Freemasons worked for society's betterment, and all the charity organizations they operated and worked through were an expression of this benevolence.

Sylvain revealed that the Grand Lodge they were part of was co-ed, meaning that women were admitted, and this was the norm worldwide. Only certain jurisdictions were exclusively men. These were things that made just enough sense at the time. It wasn't until much later that I discovered all these organizations were merely front operations designed to conceal the inner workings of the Craft.

Yes, they did lots of charity work, it's true. But a lot of those funds went toward organizations that other Masons operated.

Some of them were private and not transparent with their use of funds. One such organization, Prisma, was owned and operated by Denis; remember him? More on this later.

They painted themselves in a very positive light and seemed like nice people. They told me things I needed to hear to assuage my concerns. When I got home, I pulled out my questionnaire and filled it out; it was interesting. The first question on the list was: "Why do you want to become a Freemason?"

Uh, hello, I didn't. You were propositioning me! You kept your existence largely secret and proceeded to reel me in with tantalizing snippets of occult information. While it tempted me to write that, I thought back to my meeting and how it had gone so well, and the people were so welcoming and friendly. I wanted to do some good in society, and I wanted to be a better person. Freemasonry seemed like the ideal means to accomplish that, and that's what I wrote.

Another question was: "What can you bring to Freemasonry?" I hadn't thought about that. What did they need that I could provide? They were vague about their organization, structure, members, and requirements. I was disciplined, hard-working, relatively intelligent, and loyal. In practical terms, I was a self-employed artist and didn't know if any such skills were useful to them.

Among the requirements was the applicant's full name as it appears on their birth certificate, which I thought was odd in its specificity, along with the customary date of birth, address, and phone number you'd expect. There was a separate paper, a questionnaire, and one question was about Jesus: "What do you know about Jesus, and what does he mean to you?"

It had been a long time since I'd thought about Jesus. I just hadn't taken the time to investigate Him further. I had bits and pieces that I could recall from my childhood catechism, a positive overview. Something was reassuring about the Freemasons acknowledging and exalting Jesus. However, I didn't know that their Jesus wasn't necessarily the Biblical One, the One His Disciples knew, and Whose words and miracles were recorded based on first-hand experience. The Masonic Jesus turned out to be just another idol and, worse yet, a deceptive ruse to ease the conscience of anyone vaguely familiar with Christianity.

The last question was: "Do you believe in God?" That seemed redundant, seeing as they had just asked me about Jesus. Wasn't He God made flesh? I told myself that not everyone was Christian, so the parsing of the question made sense considering Muslims, Hindus, Sikhs, or applicants from other faiths. The reality would be very different. With time, I discovered that the Masonic Jesus was merely a prophet, another Mohammed, a good guy, but not God. Since the details of Christianity's doctrine were so far from my awareness then, I didn't think too much of it. Had I known that the Masons actually worshipped Lucifer, the god of the dark light, I would have bolted right then!

The Craft scrutinized and carefully probed the applicant. Aside from the routine criminal background check, the essay questions reveal the applicant's level of awareness and understanding. At this point, they would likely weed out someone who asked lots of hard questions, questioned the Craft's shallow explanations and motives, or had a solid commitment to their faith. This was not the end of the evaluation, however. Not even close.

Franco and I dutifully filled in our application forms and included the requisite passport-format pictures. Prisma organized a charity event at a Sugar Shack south of Montreal, the proceeds of which, we were told, would go to the disenfranchised...whatever that meant. We attended, which allowed us to hand in our applications.

After everyone had thoroughly over-eaten, and the more energetic people started taking to the dance floor, Maryse approached me and took me aside; she wanted to know if it was a good time to ask me some questions. I replied in the affirmative, so she and I took a stroll into the cool spring night on the grounds of the Sugar Shack. While everyone else made merry back inside, we discreetly discussed my application for this super secretive order. The obvious reason was that this would be part of the evaluation process now that I had submitted my application. I was to be interviewed and probed based on the answers I had provided just a few hours ago. The whole thing had the makings of a James Bond spy novel.

Maryse was very easygoing with her questions, but I don't think I've ever experienced so many awkward pauses in such a short period. I wasn't particularly nervous, just at a loss for words. The questions ended up being the same ones on the application, and for reasons I can't quite explain, I was drawing blanks, much to Maryse's dismay.

To her credit, she tried to ease me into it and started reading my answers to see if I agreed with them, which I did. The whole thing lasted only twenty minutes but felt like an hour. When we finished, Maryse told me that was all for now and that she would contact me in the coming days. Frankly, I thought I'd bombed catastrophically and was sure this would be the last I'd hear of her and Freemasonry.

Much to my surprise, several days later, I received a letter addressed to my name as it appears on my birth certificate. Upon opening it, I discovered high-quality letterhead paper from the Grand Lodge of Canada. I was flabbergasted! They extended a formal invitation to attend a Masonic orientation meeting, to be held in Laval about two weeks later.

Not only had my candidacy been accepted, but they told me I'd passed all the background checks.

Yes, I'd come up clean in their research: I had no criminal record, no history of drug use, and was in good standing in my community. Most importantly, I was someone who wasn't an immediate threat to the Lodge, and they wanted money. My money, and lots of it! It's never quite what they tell you.

Why do you think Freemasons are so involved in fundraising? They were a small, irregular Lodge looking to expand, and the administration members had voracious appetites. Regardless of its goal, every significant organization has overhead: rent, utilities, travel expenses, salaries, etc. But most reputable fraternal organizations are up-front about where the funds go and don't insist on cash with no receipts—the reason became clear much later. For now, I had a date with the Lodge that came with a $200 membership fee.

CHAPTER 6
JUST THE BEGINNING

The next step in my march toward the gates of Hell was a formal orientation meeting, to which they had invited all approved applicants. They held the meeting in Laval, at the posh home of a well-to-do brotherhood member, who I later learned was a Sovereign Grand Inspector General, which everyday folks call a 33rd-degree Mason. The event called for formal attire: a black suit, tie, and white shirt. There were at least 15 applicants, including myself and Franco, along with Denis, Maryse, Sylvain, and some other "brothers and sisters" I had yet to meet.

The orientation itself was a relaxed affair; they performed a little opening ritual, then Denis and Maryse showed us the regalia of the Lodge and how to wear it. A lodge member gave a brief testimony about the greatness of the Craft. They hadn't yet issued us our regalia as per the regulations. Once all the formalities were over, Maryse called each of us separately to see her in a small office.

The meeting lasted a few minutes, in which they asked me to say the phrase: "I would like to proceed." She accepted our payments, which covered our initiation and regalia fees and our membership dues for the next year. The price was $200, an amount designed to be just high enough to convince neophytes that they're getting something valuable, yet not so high as to dissuade people with tight purse strings from asking for a receipt. Later, they increased the yearly membership fee to $400 after the neophyte had bathed in the Craft and become comfortable. They also added other fees, such as new regalia, new initiations, and dinners.

When business had concluded, they invited us upstairs to a banquet where we hobnobbed with other members over cocktails and snacks. It felt like a stereotypical Italian wedding reception with too much food, hard liquor, and groups of people discussing "secret" things that we "new guys" weren't privy to.

Some members who'd been around for a while spoke with us. As the conversation advanced, they told us stories about how they came to the Craft and how much they enjoyed it. They also made every attempt to show off their proficiency in the cryptic, secretive code of Freemasons, knowing that we wouldn't understand a thing.

Sylvain had joined us and relished the opportunity to flaunt his understanding of the Masonic code: a series of specific questions and answers that might seem benign to casual listeners but allowed Masons to identify each other in everyday gatherings, unbeknownst to everyone else. The French term for this code is *tuilage*.

When I look back on it now, the whole was reminiscent of the "secret squirrel" mindset: we are the elite of society, we know things you don't, we have access to knowledge you don't, and we plan to keep it that way. And this was just the beginning.

About a week after the orientation meeting, I received another letter that matched my acceptance letter announcing my formal initiation, set for June 5th, 2011. This time it would be at the Masonic Lodge, on Parthenais Street in Montreal. It had all gone so fast that it felt oddly like a dream. I was excited yet apprehensive. None of us knew what to expect—this is by design.

In the days leading up to our initiation, Sylvain decided to have some fun and sent Franco and me YouTube video links with titles such as "Freemasonry Exposed" and "Secret Masonic Ritual Revealed!" Some were laughable; others were sensational; I would soon discover one was eerily accurate to what I was about to experience. The video in question can still be found online and is a French film from the forties entitled "Occult Forces.[1]" I later discovered that the film's writer, director, and producer were all purged for their involvement in the film.

Sylvain enjoyed toying with us, particularly Franco, who was quite nervous and paranoid about the initiation. I didn't understand why he had sent us that video. It was as though the Holy Spirit moved upon Sylvain, using his perverse delight to convey a blueprint for what Freemasonry was really about.

Just because someone is a wicked heathen doesn't mean they can't be useful to God. How many times has the Lord used morally dubious people to do His Will? Consider Jacob/Israel, Pharaoh, King Saul, Ahab, Nebuchadnezzar, and King Cyrus, to name a few.

God is the undefeatable Master of improv. He'll take what the enemy means for evil and turn it for good.

CHAPTER 7
MY INITIATION

I later realized that building fear in the neophytes was part of the initiation process.

June 5th, 2011 was an unusually warm Sunday. I donned my best suit and fancy watch and headed out for my date with destiny. Familiar faces greeted me at the specified address. The Lodge itself was a converted studio inside a commercial building, very unlike some of the more lavish temples I've seen over the internet, but apparently, this was the norm.

We were asked to step into a coat room and remove all articles of jewelry. They made us wait after ushering us back into the hallway. After twenty minutes, someone came out with papers and pencils and handed them to us. It was another essay questionnaire. There might have been three or four questions; I don't recall exactly.

Two of those questions were:

1. What is the primary cause?
2. What is the primary principle?

I did not know what either question meant. I didn't recall any of these things being mentioned in my conversations with Sylvain and a few others, so I left the sheet blank. To my surprise, Denis stepped out of the Lodge and into the hallway to gather our papers, asking us for some form of I.D. Everyone handed over a Medicare card or driver's license, but not me. I didn't have anything with me—Nada!

Denis paused with concern, asking me in a calm, lawyer-like demeanor, "Listen, friend; you're going to go through some potentially traumatic experiences in there. What if you suffer a heart attack or something? What should we do if something like that happens to you?"

Almost instinctively, I replied, "I dunno, call 9-1-1? Looks like there's some sort of medical facility across the street. If I don't make it, just roll my corpse over to them and tell 'em you found me this way."

I really wasn't expecting to say that; it came out almost automatically. Denis seemed so surprised that my words left him speechless, and that was no small feat! After a pregnant pause, he stepped back and quietly said, "Very well, then." He retreated into the Lodge with our papers and I.D. cards. A couple of women came out and placed a full-face blindfold on each of us. The wait continued, but now we couldn't see.

They guided a member into the Lodge periodically, and the process repeated. Finally, it was my turn. Someone gently took me by the arm and guided me through the door into a noisy, hot, and humid place where I stood in place for what seemed like forever. I heard a door ahead of me open and close, and someone was speaking loudly behind it, but I couldn't make out the details. Then, some people approached me and began taking off my jacket and unbuttoning my shirt.

I heard a woman's voice whisper, "This is part of the initiation." To be frank, I was more relieved than concerned; it was so hot in there that I welcomed it. Someone else was removing one of my shoes and socks, turning up my pant leg, and tying something to it like a rope. Despite not being able to see or tell exactly what was going on, I remained calm and focused.

They ushered me into another room., Judging by the echo, it sounded much larger than where I had just come from. A loud voice said, "Brother, who is this person?"

Someone close to me answered, "This man seeks to be inducted into our Lodge."

Another man, even more rough sounding, like a police interrogator, someone you might imagine pistol-whipping a suspect in some noir crime drama, called out my name. But I said nothing, so he repeated himself even louder. "That's me," I replied. In a booming, aggressive tone, he asked me, "What is the primary cause?"

I answered, "I don t know. They asked that on the questionnaire, but I didn't write anything."

He asked, "What is the primary principle?"

I answered, "Once again, I don t know."

He asked, "Is it your intention to infiltrate our fraternity to learn our secrets?"

I replied, "No, I don t think so."

He went on, "Tell us about your flaws."

I paused, not knowing what to say, and all that came out was, "Uhh…"

Another voice interrupted, which I recognized as Denis, saying, "Sir, there are three hundred people here observing and taking notes. Do you think you're taking this seriously enough?"

I felt anxious for a second, and then as if on cue, a little voice came from somewhere deep down and said, "They're just trying to rattle your cage." With that, as quickly as the anxiety came, it subsided.

The interrogator continued, "So, about your flaws?"

This time I answered, "Right, well, I can be a bit of a workaholic, and I have a temper, and…"

He interrupted, asking, "Are we going to have problems with you?"

To which I sarcastically replied, "Why, do you want to?"

Whatever this was, or was supposed to be, probably wasn't having the desired effect because Denis then exclaimed, "Who recommended this candidate?"

I heard Sylvain's voice in an apologetic tone say, "I did, Grand Master, and I offer you my most sincere apologies."

Another voice, one I didn't recognize, said, "I think we've heard enough. Brother, take the candidate underground to the Cabinet of reflection. Let him pause and consider what has transpired here."

Once again, that calming little voice from within chimed in, saying, "It's just a bluff, don't be afraid." And so, I wasn't.

They ushered me up and down some steps and sat me in an uncomfortable chair. At that point, my blindfold was removed. I found myself in a small room that was painted black and illuminated by a single candle. On the walls were phrases like, "If you're here by curiosity, go away!" Along with other such welcoming sentences.

Directly in front of me was a small table with a few objects: what looked like salt, water, a piece of bread, and a small rooster, among other trinkets. I wasn't afraid or concerned, but quite fascinated by all the symbolism and what they made me go through. Overwhelmed by curiosity, I almost forgot I was sweating bullets from the heat and humidity. I reasoned that the theatrical performance I'd been part of was a sentencing, and I was now dead and buried.

The total experience in the Cabinet of Reflection lasted about two or three minutes. A woman entered the room, placed my blindfold back on, and asked me if I wanted to continue, to which I answered yes. They escorted me to another location, where they dipped my hands in water and passed them over an open flame. I heard some loud shouts, and they gave me a beverage. I first thought this was terrible wine, only to realize it was probably vinegar.

It made sense; the entire experience mirrored life: you don t know where you're going, you stagger clumsily over obstacles throughout life, and life is often bitter. I was told to place my right hand on someone's shoulder and became part of a convoy, with people ahead of me and behind, as we marched in circles for who knows how long.

After going through several other obstacles, including a low door, a seesaw, having a candle put out on my back, and having ponderous chains placed about our necks and then taken off, our blindfolds were removed. We found ourselves in what turned out to be the middle of the Lodge, with Freemasons behind us and in front of us, holding swords pointed directly at us. A man whose voice I recalled from earlier was the Worshipful Master of the Lodge, who explained what was happening: we were to take an oath.

While the exact wording escapes me, part of the oath involved keeping the secrets of my fellow brothers and sisters; that betraying my oath meant I would have my throat slit from ear-to-ear; and that there may come a time when I could expect to shed every drop of my blood to protect my fellow brothers and sisters and Freemasonry as a whole.

A blood-curdling oath for sure; I will not deny it. I will disclose, however, that before we proceeded, Denis interjected, explaining that the oath we were about to take was not a literal one; no one would slit our throats or anything of that nature; the oath itself was purely symbolic. Having your throat slit meant that if we breached our oath for any reason, we would be energetically cut off from the egregore of the Lodge. Frankly, we were so exhausted from our trials that most just wanted to go home, shower, and go to bed.

Before concluding, an Officer of the Lodge took us aside, to show us the cursory Entered Apprentice grip, transmit the mystic word to us, demonstrate how to wear our aprons, and explain the basic do's and don'ts of Masonic life. We received a Masonic I.D. card with our name, photo & rank, our Entered Apprentice diploma, and some small booklets describing the ritual we had just undergone.

Once assigned a specific Lodge, the last thing given to us was a small yellow card that had a daily prayer on one side and, on the reverse, a different prayer they encouraged us to read on Saturdays.

Well, that was all very interesting!

CHAPTER 8
THE CURTAIN PULLED BACK

After a shower and changing clothes at home, I started feeling uneasy. It was as if I'd done something bad, and I couldn't shake the feeling of dread that had come over me. I repeatedly went over the events in my mind. All the symbols, strange rituals, and that creepy oath. I started having second thoughts about what I'd just gotten myself into, and for a moment, I wasn't sure if I wanted to go back. I eventually did, but I promised myself something first: I'd play along, at least for now, but if I saw or heard anything that violated my conscience, I was out!

Before going any further, I want to clarify the Entered Apprentice ritual you just read about. While you can find books that enumerate and explain all the symbols and give you the "official" meanings, I'll tell you what most Masons don't understand and what the ones who do won't tell you.

The entire initiation ritual and its lead-up is a psychological operation designed to destabilize the neophyte. Based on my conversations with the Grand Master, as well as my research, the

Entered Apprentice initiation aims to get the proverbial "hamster" in the neophyte's head to run in overdrive. Once their sense of discernment is destroyed, carefully bring them back into a calm state—much like Plato's Cave—the shadows, sensations, and sounds are all honed to create a false impression through the use of elaborate theatrics.

As an illustration, the penal sign (salute) of the Entered Apprentice is essentially the same movement as "slitting one's throat": raise the right hand, placing the thumb on the left side of one's throat with the four other fingers straightened and together, then dragging the thumb across to the right side and merging all five fingers into a primitive pentagram to complete the gesture, then bring the arm back down naturally to one's side.

This movement reminds the Mason that he stands under oath to have his throat slit, metaphorically speaking, should he betray his oath. The Entered Apprentice (E.A.) initiation starts by metaphorically severing the head from the heart, representing the loss of discernment, then recovering it. While that's bad enough, what happens in between is far more insidious.

While some may think this is all just a harmless charade, I assure you it is not. By their own admission, Freemasons work with "spirit guides" and use theatrics to divert their brothers and sisters so that those guides can work on us. On page 104 of *They Shall Expel Demons*[1], written by Derek Prince, a renowned Pentecostal Pastor and deliverance Minister, he states clearly that involvement in the occult is one way demons enter people. Just a little further, on page 106, he discusses how emotional shock, fear, or sustained pressure is another way evil spirits can enter someone. This will make sense shortly.

By the grace of God, I wasn't successfully fooled by what was going on, but I assure you that many people were.

Once you've "passed through" the initiation, the Lodge encourages Masons to attend subsequent E.A. initiations as spectators to get a different perspective and learn the proverbial ropes. One day, they might be elected as Lodge Officers and conduct the ceremony for future neophytes.

Many people undergoing the trials of the E.A. initiation are utterly confused and distraught. On one occasion, the Worshipful Master saw that the neophyte was on the verge of panic and frantically gestured to the interrogator to tone it down. The candidate is shown and allowed to overhear things that mess with their mind: the deliberate asking of I.D., the mention of potential health issues, intentionally depriving them of their primary sense (sight), being barked at, jeered, and derided by unseen prosecutors, then after a very brief pause, made to undergo a series of trials in rapid succession engenders confusion and keeps the victim off-balance.

The basics of the ceremony are the same as those used by interrogators in less civilized parts of the world to encourage collaboration and get confessions; this alone should send red flags and warning signals to your mind.

As an E.A. Freemason, you're expected to attend at least one monthly meeting called a "Blue Lodge" (B.L.) meeting. Additionally, there are "White Lodge" (W.L.) meetings: optional gatherings similar to B.L. meetings, but with a curtailed opening and closing ceremony and a much more relaxed, informal ambiance. They're more like study groups, where you can ask questions, take notes, and learn the ins and outs of rituals, initiations, and other elements of Masonic protocol.

As someone who doesn't like to do things half-assed, I decided it was my duty as a Mason to learn as much as possible about the Craft and help my fellow brothers and sisters in their journeys.

This meant attending every meeting I could, reading as much recommended literature as possible, and becoming proficient. As such, I made it a point to attend W.L. meetings whenever possible.

Another reason most people within the Craft have a false sense of security about all the questionable symbolism and rituals is the presence of the "Volume of the Sacred Law" upon the altar, in front of and below the Worshipful Master. In the Ancient and Accepted Scottish Rite, that Volume of the Sacred Law is none other than the Holy Bible. Not some special Masonic Bible: the regular version you can get from any bookstore. We were also asked to kiss the Bible three times before taking our oath as part of our initiation ritual, something that might very well assuage the fears of some, but all is not what it seems.

The Lodge, which I was a part of, Zenith Lodge number 2, made it part of their opening ritual for the Chaplain to read John 1:1-13, which is a wonderful thing—in the proper context. Sadly, the Jesus of Freemasonry is merely a prophet and not God. They hold a Gnostic (heretical) view of the Scriptures, but if you don't study and familiarize yourself with the Word of God, you probably won't pick up on it. They know who the God of the Bible (Hashem) is; they merely don't worship Him. For even the Scriptures tell us:

> *You believe that God is one; you do well. Even the demons believe—*
> *and shudder!*

> —JAMES 2:19(ESV)

CHAPTER 9
THE CABINET OF REFLECTION

Remember that little black room I mentioned earlier, the Cabinet of Reflection? I had spent just a short amount of time there during my initiation, a time far too brief and thoroughly distracted by the preceding events to gauge the situation properly. It was only much later that I understood what that little out-of-the-way room really was.

One such W.L. meeting was particularly revealing. It must have been shortly after I'd been "raised" to the degree of Master Mason. By this time, my Worshipful Master (Lodge President) had already been promoted to the rank of Grand Master (Master of the Grand Lodge). He was habitually present at W.L. meetings, not only to monitor us but also to impart his knowledge and experience. The subject of the evening was the Cabinet of Reflection, and they invited us to revisit it, free of all the emotional and mental distractions that had permeated our initiation. The experience was eye-opening.

Stepping into it, you could feel something bizarre, as though you were stepping into a different dimension, and the natives of that dimension were observing you. It was subtle, but you couldn't help noticing when you were in a calm state. Later, when the Grand Master asked us what we felt when we stepped in there, I volunteered to answer, explaining what I described above. He congratulated me on my perceptiveness and confirmed that the Cabinet of Reflection was indeed a portal, a gateway to the underworld.

As part of our initiation, we were intentionally escorted into a portal and exposed to the dark side so those entities could size us up and provide what was needed to mold us into what they wanted.

Wow!

The Grand Master further elaborated, stating that the Cabinet of Reflection was considered the heart or the furnace of every Grand Lodge and fundamental to the existence of the Lodge itself. Denis also divulged this in a slightly more subtle manner, himself a Past Grand Master, during one of his "Prisma" conferences. He drew the parallel between Freemasonry and the ancient Egyptian mystery schools and how a portal to the dark side was intentionally opened so the candidate would be exposed to it.

So just in case you blanked out and missed it, the Grand Master *and* Past Grand Master confirmed, from their lips to my ears, that Freemasonry willingly and knowingly exposes newcomers to evil spirits and that it's a fundamental part of the Masonic process. Let that sink in.

Now I know what you're thinking: "Why in the bloody blue blazes didn't you just run the heck out of there?" Understand that what you're now reading resulted from countless hours of research, condensing data points, snippets of conversations, information amassed from various sources, and testimony gathered over several years; then synthesized and condensed into several dozen pages for your convenient reading.

The reason most "regular" Masonic Lodges don't want to promote members too quickly and have caps on how many Masons can rise to the next level per year is to maintain secrecy. The frog needs to be boiled slowly and carefully. If one hurries the process and exposes the new Mason to too much shocking information too quickly, they may discover the nature of the organization and bolt.

This is also why each degree is compartmentalized, and a heavy premium is placed on secrecy and discretion. Masons of higher rank are forbidden to share the secrets of their degree with those lower on the ladder; they scrutinize even casual conversations. Masons are encouraged to snitch when a fellow Mason slips up. I was not only a witness to this, but to my great shame, I took part in it as well.

It reminds me of what life must have been like in Eastern Europe before the fall of the Iron Curtain—constantly observed in your casual conversations, on social media, and at public gatherings. Although there are no abductions and no one gets arrested, you can expect a stern talking-to from your Worshipful Master and a condescending attitude from your fellow Masons, just enough to keep you in line.

None of this happens at first; they don't want to reveal the game until a Mason is sufficiently immersed in the order's culture. By then, most are committed and it's part of their lives. The things that happen slowly and those that happen quickly are all by design; either the intent is to move so quickly in order to cause confusion or so slowly as not to trigger your inner alarm. The intention is always to hide what they think you're not ready to see.

In fact, neophytes are usually "love bombed" by fellow members when they're new. On the day of my E.A. initiation, once all the important stuff was squared away, we were invited to a banquet where we could get refreshments and discuss our experiences with fellow members.

This banquet is held after every initiation and Lodge meeting and is called the "agape." During this feast, many members will come and congratulate you on your "graduation," complete with handshakes and hugs. The sentiments conveyed are most likely sincere; these, by themselves, are not a problem. The issue is the intentional secrecy and, as I later discovered, the rank hypocrisy of those in positions of authority—more on this later.

A last detail worthy of mention occurred during this banquet. Upon retrieving my watch, keys, and the amber pendant Denis had given me some months back, a fellow sister noticed the latter as I placed it around my neck and immediately stopped me. Surprised, she asked me where I'd gotten that pendant, so I told her. She wanted to see it, and I happily obliged. It was quite an odd sight watching this middle-aged woman cradling this little piece of amber in her hands; you'd think I had handed her some priceless artifact that she'd longed for her whole life. I asked her what was so special about it, and she simply said that I must be someone extraordinary to receive something like this.

Uh… What?

She didn't elaborate, and I was too tired to pursue the topic further, but I think you can see how neophytes are made to feel special...very special. They build you up until your head is in the clouds, and when the time is right, and you're least expecting it, they pull the rug out from under you! The reason will become clear later.

I was adjusting to my new Masonic identity, and I decided I was going to attempt the Saturday prayer printed on that little yellow card for the first time. What could go wrong?

CHAPTER 10
DARK SHADOWS

The prayers seemed like a good thing. I had already recited the daily version a few times, and everything had gone well. I hadn't fully memorized it, so I satisfied myself by just reading it off the card until I became comfortable reciting it. For reasons I didn't understand, there was a specific Saturday prayer that was different. I didn't think too much of it, so when Saturday evening rolled around, I took a seat in my comfy chair, grabbed my little yellow card, and began reciting. That's when I noticed it.

Out of the corner of my right eye, I saw movement! Not a speck of light or a shape necessarily; what I saw was more like the mirage effect you see on asphalt on a hot summer day. This distortion appeared at roughly head height, just a few feet off to my right side. Fascinated and curious, I wondered if the distortion related to the prayer, something random, or merely an optical illusion. The rest of that evening was uneventful, but I noted what had transpired, just in case.

At our next Lodge meeting a couple of weeks later, I was chatting with Franco and remembered the strange distortion, so I mentioned it to him. To my surprise, he had experienced the same thing when he recited the Saturday prayer! We seemed to have activated something supernatural and couldn't help thinking that maybe we'd done something wrong. Thinking we needed tech support regarding this anomaly, I sought a Brother who was a Royal Arch Mason (13th degree), since he had more experience under his belt. But he confessed experiencing nothing of that nature. In fact, he told us that the prayer cards were relatively recent, and he and his wife, who was also a Mason, hadn't ever received them.

Disappointed, I dropped the matter. It was wiser to take a wait-and-see approach; see if the phenomenon occurred again, and if it did, I'd press someone else for answers.

It didn't happen again, but other things did.

Not too long after that strange phenomenon, I got into some heated quarrels with my dad. My relationship with him had always been tenuous, but it suddenly felt as though a switch had been flipped. Out of the blue, he'd provoke an argument about something trivial. Sometimes I'd just walk away, but other times I'd get angry at his provocation and fire back, escalating the situation. It started up rather suddenly, came in short bursts, then things went calm almost as quickly as it fired up. I didn't correlate it with any supernatural phenomena I had experienced; that came much later.

Despite those temper flares, things seemed to return to normal for the next 16 months. Things in the Lodge were going well. As part of Masonic protocol, they assign Entered Apprentices a "godfather" or "godmother," a senior Mason who can mentor them and help them progress throughout their Masonic career. While I had originally selected Sylvain for that task, the Worshipful Master of the Lodge reckoned Sylvain didn't have enough experience, as he was only one degree higher than I was.

I asked another brother, a Royal Arch Mason, and he accepted. He mentored me for about a month before unexpectedly telling me I might be better off with someone more experienced in the Craft.

As luck would have it, my Worshipful Master, who we will call Pierre, volunteered to be godfather to both Franco and me. I should mention that he also served as our interrogator during our initiation. A heavy-set man in his late fifties, Pierre had been a career police officer and detective, and it showed—his short-cropped hair; his beady, piercing eyes; the way he carried himself; and the way he addressed people just oozed with intimidation. In his younger days, I imagined him slamming a suspect's head into a car door and writing it off as a procedural malfunction in his paperwork.

Yeah, that type of cop.

While the prospect didn't thrill me, he was certainly qualified and had decades of experience in the Craft. We had learned shortly after initiation that Pierre was a Sovereign Grand Inspector General and had, according to Denis, unlocked some of the secret degrees—those above the 33rd. For better or for worse, he'd be supervising us, and I resigned to making the best of it.

As part of our Masonic "duty," members of the Craft, especially newer members, must create pieces of architecture: a fancy way of referring to a research paper on a Masonic topic. We were expected to produce a minimum of three such works over the course of a Masonic year. For those who aren't aware, the Masonic year begins in September and ends in late June. As a point of clarification, it's not that Freemasons use some bizarre form of timekeeping; rather, think of Freemasonry as a kind of university of "higher learning." Just as most learning institutions take summer break, so do the occult orders.

While the policy on pieces of architecture wasn't strictly enforced, those papers, which could be as short as two or three pages, were excellent opportunities to research and learn. Like everything else in Freemasonry, the papers had a hidden meaning. On the one hand, the papers, which were submitted to the Worshipful Master and shared with our godfather, allowed the writer an opportunity to learn about and discuss various Masonic topics and permitted our godfather to track our progress. The flip side of that coin was that the papers would also give those in positions of authority insight into what we were reading, learning, and understanding.

It was frowned upon for Masons to venture beyond the confines of their present degree. The official explanation being that the current degree already holds enough material to cover and learn, and that advancing too quickly could lead to confusion. The Mason, through this process, is slowly being acclimatized to function within a box. Where do you think these government spy agencies learned to structure and compartmentalize their organizations? It's entirely possible to have co-workers that you've known for years, work in the same department, one cubicle over, yet they take part in projects that you do not know of. This is precisely how Freemasonry operates, and the guys on the bottom rungs are oblivious to it.

So how did I learn these things, you ask? Aside from hosting private spiritual conferences through Prisma, Denis, the Past

Grand Master of the Lodge, was also offering spiritual weekend workshops to both Masons and non-Masons alike. These 3-day events were usually held in a secluded hostel North of Montreal and were more elaborate and in-depth versions of his monthly conferences. While most of the information turned out to be nothing more than nonsense, he was also mixing-in secrets from the higher Masonic degrees. They encouraged us to take part in these workshops, being told they would help us "travel up the ladder" of the order more quickly.

Now I know what you're thinking: did I not, just earlier, tell you that the Lodge discouraged people from learning the secrets of higher degrees prematurely? Did I not also explain that there were quotas preventing members from being promoted too quickly? Of course, I did, but here's where this already convoluted story becomes a tangled mess!

The Grand Lodge of Canada came to find out in time that Mr. Denis, Sovereign Grand Inspector General, Past Grand Master, and President of Prisma, was disclosing higher-echelon Masonic secrets to the profane (the uninitiated) for profit.

If you're confused, good, you should be. All of this will make sense later, but for the time being, please remember these three important principles:

1. Freemasonry is an order within an order;
2. There is no honor among thieves;
3. The dark side always consumes its own.

Let us journey back to the fall of 2011: I was a newly initiated, proud Freemason, and I was hungry for knowledge. I was still attending the monthly spiritual conferences hosted by Prisma, besides the Lodge meetings. You might wonder why I was still bothering with those now that I was on the inside. The answer was simple: aside from all the pomp and ceremony of the opening and closing rituals of your average B.L. meeting, not a lot of knowledge was being dispensed there. In fact, the meetings themselves were uneventful.

CHAPTER II
LODGE WORKINGS

Now comes the juicy stuff that so many people have asked me: what are these Blue Lodge meetings like, and what happens there? Brace yourself; you're about to be underwhelmed! The average Blue Lodge meeting goes something like this:

- Everyone gathers in a separate room adjacent to the temple, called the courtyard. This is where people change their clothes, have a quick snack, adjust their regalia, and take some quiet time for themselves, leaving behind their worldly cares as they prepare to enter the "sacred" space that is the Lodge. During this time, the Lodge Officers, including the Master of Ceremony, are in the Lodge itself, making preparations behind closed doors.
- Once the people in the adjacent room have made their preparations, the Master of Ceremony (a dude or dudette with a long staff) comes to gather them. The Masons are escorted into the Lodge in groups according

to their rank. Once all the Masons are seated, everyone stands, and the Officers perform the cryptic and symbolic opening ceremony. I won't delve into the details, but if you'd like a more in-depth explanation of what happens and why, they can be found in "Mysteres et actions du rituel d'ouverture en loge Magonnique" by Alain Pozarnik. It's a long, dreary, and absurdly elaborate breakdown of the Blue Lodge opening ritual, and lucky for you, it's in French! Truthfully, I don't recommend buying or reading anything of an occult nature.

- When the opening ritual is over, the Worshipful Master takes his seat in the East, and the snooze-fest begins.

- A Lodge Officer—I forget which one—takes attendance. When they call your name, you're expected to stand and salute while uttering, "Present to the light of this temple."

- The Worshipful Master gives everyone a run-down on upcoming events, changes to the calendar, initiation date changes, upcoming visitors, and things of this nature.

- The Worshipful Master, along with the Lodge Secretary, bring up motions that the Lodge members must vote on: confirmation of the amount received in donations in the last month, the monthly expense budget, who's assigned to take out the trash, organize the banquets, etc.

- A brother or sister will usually present and read a piece of architecture to the Lodge. Then the Lodge members ask questions and/or debate the topic presented.

- The meeting winds down when the Officers pass the collection basket to gather donations and written suggestions from Lodge members, very similar to what you see in church.

- The Officers perform the closing ceremony, after which
  all the Lodge members gather in the adjacent room,
  which also serves as the outer court of the temple, for
  the banquet and small talk.

That, my friends, is it. I know, super exciting, right?

The White Lodge meetings are marginally more informative since these are held primarily for the first three degrees. As an E.A., you're only exposed to information pertinent to that degree. What they disclosed during the Prisma conferences was far more informative and practical than anything revealed in the Lodge, so I made it a point to attend the Prisma conferences. Those conferences were launching pads for spiritual weekend workshops and were organized by theme.

One theme that stuck out to me was the Knights Templar formation, which was held over four weekends, each about a month apart with the last weekend being one long initiation. We were casually told that the formation was the equivalent of the Knight Kadosh (30th) degree of Freemasonry and that these weekend workshops would help a Mason advance more quickly through the ranks. Since I already had a soft spot for the knights of old, I signed up. Like the conferences and the order itself, they shrouded the course curriculum and contents in mystery, but that was all according to plan. Remember, Freemasonry was still very new to me at this stage.

That these conferences divulged secrets in violation of the Masonic constitution was unknown to me. As far as I was concerned, Denis was the Grand Master of the Lodge, and both he and Maryse were 33rds. I figured they knew what they were doing and that it was on the level. What could have been their motivation for betraying the order? Money! Is it not written in the Bible that the love of money is the root of all evil?

At this time, the Grand Lodge of Canada was undertaking steps to join forces with an international organization called CLIPSAS (Centre de Liaison et d'Information des Puissances maçonniques Signataires de l'Appel de Strasbourg.) Not all Masonic Lodges are equal: to be considered a "regular" Masonic Lodge, you must conform to certain standards. Technically, absolutely anyone can start their own Masonic Lodge, but they refer to these as "wild" or "irregular" Lodges. By joining an international body like CLIPSAS, the administration hoped to get a certain legitimacy, but there was another reason. One which Denis did not hide.

During one Grand Lodge meeting, Denis openly stated that his intent for joining the CLIPSAS was to infiltrate it. He wanted "our people" in positions of authority and to transform it from within to reflect our (or rather Denis') vision of what Freemasonry should be. Remember this for later and remember what I said about there being no honor among thieves.

To be accepted into this body, verifications were needed. Inspectors attended our Lodge meetings to verify whether our rituals conformed to international standards and to identify what changes were required for membership. After much back-and-forth negotiation, the inspectors came. Oddly enough, Pierre briefed us on our visiting inspectors and how to "handle" them. The inspection group came from New York in the U.S.; we were a French-speaking Lodge.

Despite many of us being fluent in both languages, they urged us to play dumb and pretend that our English wasn't so good. We were also told that the inspectors would intentionally try to trip us up, so the less we said, the better.

When the inspectors arrived, the meeting turned out to be far more pleasant than any of us expected. The bad news came shortly after that, indirectly from the Inspectors through the Grand Lodge Officers. who then transmitted the results to us. A member of the **CLIPSAS** board was familiar with Denis, and there were some issues between them. According to Pierre, this person had it in for Denis and blocked our acceptance into the organization.

As for what that personal row between Denis and CLIPSAS member Elie was about, we'll get to that much later, and it's a doozy!

On Christmas morning that same year, I experienced an unusual phenomenon. It was a little past midnight, and I was at my computer. The T.V. to my left was off, and the room was dark, illuminated by my computer screen directly in front of me and my lit Christmas tree far off to the right and behind me. Suddenly, and for barely a second, the entire room shone brightly, as if someone had taken a picture with a flash. Out of the corner of my eye, I saw two orbs of pure, white light, about the size of bowling balls, move from left to right across my living room ceiling and then disappeared into it.

Had I blinked or not been looking in that direction when it occurred, I would likely have missed it. I had seen nothing like that before. That phenomenon has only recurred twice in the years since and was never as dramatic as that first occurrence.

While I strongly suspect that these orbs were spiritual entities, to this day, I've never been able to determine what "team" they were on. Judging by how much bigger and brighter they were, compared to the tiny specs I'd seen before, I can't help think that these were some sort of spiritual V.I.P.'s.

CHAPTER 12
THE IMITATOR

The Knights Templar workshop proved far more fascinating than anything disclosed in the Lodge or any of my recommended Masonic books. A couple of years later I'd understand that a large amount of it was convoluted nonsense dreamed up by Denis. There were still some golden nuggets of information that later proved useful; data points that connected to form an elaborate and terrifying spider web that few people in the order ever saw.

Denis was a classic narcissist. Narcissists love to brag and talk about themselves; they can't help it. They talk and talk and talk compulsively. They'll initially be careful about what they say around you, but if you don't give them any pushback, they'll let their guard down and get careless. If you train yourself to listen and maintain a calm demeanor, you can learn a lot from such people. If you're patient, it's only a matter of time until they give you the proverbial rope to hang them with. Sometimes they'll even save you the trouble and hang themselves, metaphorically speaking, of course.

During the workshop, we learned some very interesting tidbits of information about the Knights Templar, or things they believed about themselves, such as:

- There were previous iterations of Knights Templar throughout history, going back almost six thousand years.
- Several of those orders are still around and active today, including but not limited to the order of the Knights of Malta, which descends from the Knights Hospitaller.
- Freemasonry is one such order and is the synthesis of several occult orders.
- Various Templar orders have incrementally and deliberately infiltrated all of the fundamental institutions of our society, including the Catholic Church, and altered the course of these institutions to reflect the values of these respective orders.
- The Knights Templar and their cousins, the Freemasons, both employ a compartmentalized hierarchy system. As such, it is an order within an order, where the workings of the inner circle are kept secret from the outer members.
- Just as the Christian has the Armor of God at his disposal, the Templar Knight has a series of armaments: helmet, shoes, belt, sword, shield, and dagger at his disposal. These "weapons" are actual entities that the Templar can control, or believes he controls.
- The original Templar Knights "crash-landed" on earth thousands of years ago; they are *not* of human origin but passed their knowledge onto us. Denis described these beings as more-or-less like us, but their skin had a lightly luminous quality.

- If you're even remotely familiar with your Bible, you might be thinking of certain Biblical passages right about now.

Shining morning star, how you have fallen from the heavens! You destroyer of nations, you have been cut down to the ground.

— ISAIAH 14:12 (CSB)

He replied, "I saw Satan fall like lightning from heaven."

— LUKE 10:18 (NIV)

The great dragon was hurled down—that ancient serpent called the devil, or Satan, who leads the whole world astray. He was hurled to the earth, and his angels with him.

— REVELATION 12:9 (NIV)

While not part of the Canon, that same event is described in 1 Enoch, where a group of Watchers came down from Mount Hermon and decided to take human wives to create angelic-human hybrid offspring, effectively rebelling against the Lord. Those Watchers then imparted divine knowledge to man, such as the fashioning of weapons of war, the art of seduction, and other forbidden knowledge.

There were giants in the earth in those days; and also after that, when the sons of God came in unto the daughters of men, and they bare children to them, the same became mighty men which were of old, men of renown.

— GENESIS 6:4 (KJV)

Therefore, if I may be so blunt as to condense this for you: we were taught that the Knights Templar and, by extension, Freemasonry's teachings originated with fallen angels.

There, I said it!

It should come as no surprise that the occultists want to portray themselves in a positive light, and they are exceedingly skilled at doing that. Had I been more knowledgeable about Scripture at that time, I likely would have run for my life! I would have saved myself lots of pain and suffering if I had. But it didn't happen that way. I believe there were still some things the Lord wanted me to see, and if I didn't want to see them, He'd allow it to hurt until I did.

I correct and discipline those whom I love. [...]

— REVELATION 3:19 (CEB)

CHAPTER 13
THE FELLOW CRAFT DEGREE

I received my first Masonic "raise," moving up to the Fellow Craft degree. That initiation was a startling contrast to the first one: no blindfold, no psychodrama, no theatrics. In fact, it was all quite bland. While they had failed to rattle my cage as an Entered Apprentice, they would eventually come back with a vengeance when I least expected it.

While initiations themselves are open doors that allow evil spirits to enter someone at the moment, as we'll see shortly, evil can be a very subtle, creeping thing. As in any war, the kingdom of darkness has a variety of strategies. Sometimes its forces bide their time, lie in wait until an opening or opportunity presents itself, then strike without warning.

While the Entered Apprentice initiation messes with your mind, the Fellow Craft initiation jars you emotionally; not immediately, of course. From the time the first initiation takes place until the next one, the "theme" of the initiation is constantly being implemented into the Mason's life. They set things in motion in the Lodge, but they play out in your daily life, often blindsiding you.

I had the misfortune of overlapping the Fellow Craft degree and the so-called "Knights Templar" initiations. Denis, the narcissist that he was, likely took offense to my resistance to his mind games in round one. This time, he was going for payback with interest, if only to soothe his wounded pride.

The Knights Templar initiation was the most intense thing I'd experienced in my life. Unlike the formal Masonic initiations that lasted a few hours, depending on how many candidates were present, this one lasted the entire weekend! From the time we arrived on Friday evening until Sunday afternoon, we were under the gun. Denis, accompanied by Maryse and Sylvain, came out charging. They assembled us in the main conference hall and began yelling at us, claiming we were not taking our process seriously, that we were not fit to be part of the order, and that we needed to shape up if we wanted to pass this initiation.

Denis and Maryse had been gentle as doves throughout the four previous weekends; they were encouraging us, saying that we were advancing admirably. They commended us multiple times on our insight into certain teachings and model behavior. In reality, the only thing we'd done was become comfortable; we hadn't anticipated his tactics.

The rest of the weekend involved situations such as Denis deliberately dictating texts at a hurried pace, knowing full well some people would miss certain passages. If you missed parts of the dictation, you were yelled at; if you asked the person next to you for the details you missed from the dictation, you were yelled at. At one point, he walked up to one woman whose text was complete and calmly asked her if she had captured it all the first time around or asked someone for help, to which she responded that someone had helped her fill in some blanks. He calmly took her papers, his face now producing an unmistakable scowl, tore them up and tossed them to the floor in front of everyone.

Franco's ex-girlfriend had set up an online dating profile to put her acrimonious break-up behind her. Denis, Maryse, and their henchmen had sharp ears, overhearing her discuss the matter with some fellow brothers and sisters. Armed with this information, Denis confronted her before the entire assembly, lamenting and deriding her—an initiate and aspiring Templar Knight—for putting herself "on the market" in such a profane fashion. He said she was an embarrassment to the order. An event that humiliated her, bringing her to tears and utterly breaking her, she nearly stormed out of the initiation—she should have; we all should have, but we didn't.

Some of us caught on that all these trials were part of the actual initiation, and while I certainly thought it was going too far, I resigned to seeing it through. Denis calmly addressed us, saying that if anyone wanted to throw in the towel, we could do so, but that meant forfeiting our diplomas. Clearly, I was to have none of that; I wasn't about to quit. I couldn't help thinking there was a purpose to all of this, and while the flesh wanted to walk away, I opted to persevere. If you're going through hell…keep going!

Sobbing, crying people were the norm that weekend. Another trial on Saturday involved all of us being placed in a small, closed room with poor ventilation and made to wait…and wait. Then, Sylvain entered the room and seemed to pick a brother at random, telling him, "You're going first." They both exited the room, and Sylvain shut the door behind them. We could clearly hear what seemed like a violent commotion between this brother, Sylvain, and unseen people in the hallway. The brother yelled, "No, stop!" at the top of his lungs, and other inaudible screams, topped with the sounds of clanging chairs and stomps.

What the hell was happening? What on earth could have caused him to freak out like that?

The silence lasted several minutes; then Sylvain reappeared and accompanied the next candidate out. This time, there was no commotion. Gradually, every single person in the room had their turn until I was the only one left. I must have been in that room for well over an hour. I couldn't actually say because they deprived us of our phones, jewelry, and watches. As always, this was by design.

Then Sylvain came for me. My heart was racing, and as if the room itself wasn't hot and stuffy enough, I was sweating bullets, troubled by the fate that awaited me. Sylvain was nervous and evaded eye contact as they marched me down the corridor. Something happened at that moment, and fear left me. I knew not how, but I realized I would be OK.

A fellow sister wearing an unusually calm and welcoming smile took me downstairs and ushered me into a bathroom. Denis was standing by the shower and pulled the curtain aside for me. I entered, and he blasted me with a jet of cold water. I was told to keep my face in the water stream and repeat the words he uttered. He had me repeat a series of words over and over, gasping for breath as I did so, and suddenly the stream of water stopped. Then, in a seemingly futile gesture, Sylvain stooped to wipe my feet as I exited the shower, soaking wet. I later found out that he had done this for no one else, and I surmised that the guilt of the ruse he had taken part in weighed heavily on what remained of his conscience.

The brother who had gone first and put up the appearance of a struggle at the beginning of the ordeal was in cahoots with Sylvain, Denis, and Maryse. They had enlisted his help and deliberated together to concoct something that would promulgate fear in everyone, and he was quite proud of his performance.

It was mid-afternoon, and once the adrenaline had worn off, many of us were struggling to keep our eyes open, so we all took a brief nap. They then asked us to perform a series of light exercises and encouraged us to keep a journal of all that had transpired. Supper was served, then they invited several people to give their "impressions" of the events that had taken place up to that point. Many of us exchanged notes on when we realized it was all a setup. The rest of the evening was much more relaxed, but not over.

Denis awakened us around 2 a.m., ushered us out of bed, and outside into the pitch darkness and the freezing cold that was customary in mid-May. We were asked to lie on the ground on our stomachs with our faces in the dirt and concentrate on the visions we were to receive, then go back inside and write it all down. Frankly, the only thing I saw was some jumbled colors, and I couldn't wait to get back to bed. After stumbling back indoors and a quick shower to wash off the dirt from the mucky ground, it was back to bed for all of us. The ordeal for most of us was over by Sunday morning.

Troubled sleep left many in a state of lethargy. During a simple reciting exercise, Denis snapped at me for the last time that weekend, rebuking me for allowing my gaze to depart my exercise partner's gaze during the assigned task. I hadn't done anything wrong; he simply selected a moment of perceived weakness and used it to startle me. I will explain shortly the reasons for all these events.

Once the weekend's events were over, we had a late lunch, packed our things, and headed back to Montreal. Unbeknownst to me, I was experiencing the onset of a progressive nervous breakdown brought about by the intense ordeals I'd endured. Our "graduation" ceremony and diploma wouldn't come for another two months, and I was going to use that time to reflect on what I'd just gone through and what my plans would be.

CHAPTER 14
THE MASK BEGINS TO SLIP

The "initiation" I went through probably sounds like torture more than anything else, and you're correct. In fact, many of the techniques employed, such as fear, intimidation, humiliation, sleep deprivation, and pseudo-waterboarding are all recognized (and allegedly outlawed) torture techniques. If all this sounds like a lighter version of the horror stories that came out of the Guantanamo Bay scandal several years ago, you're correct. Where do you think all these big government agencies get their ideas from?

It's not merely the techniques themselves but the deliberate sequencing and timing that amplifies the effect: build a person up, break them down, build them up again by giving them hope, break them down; rinse and repeat, over and over.

Do you remember when I cited Pastor Derek Prince earlier in Chapter 8? About how emotional shock, pressure, and sustained fear allow demons to enter a person? That's precisely what was happening to us! Besides this, exposing people to alternating states of fear, hope/calm, then more fear in repeated cycles breaks people emotionally and makes them far more susceptible to suggestion. When people are fearful, they're more likely to do what they're told by an authority figure and less likely to question anything. In short, it's all about mind control and making obedient little soldiers that will do as they're told, how they're told and when they're told.

Denis, had his own ideas about how the initiation process should work. He was very vocal and candid about how he felt it was unnecessarily long and how, at this point in man's "evolution," the process should speed up, unlike traditional Freemasonry, which opts for the slow, incremental route of creating good, unquestioning, compliant soldiers, whom the order can use to carry out its purposes, avoiding a person's alarm bells. As for what kind of evidence or data he relied on to make this assertion, your guess is as good as mine. More likely, he just thought he knew better than everyone else, including the demons around which the order revolves.

There were many instances where Denis made bold claims and assertions about things I could prove were incorrect, but seeing how he exploded on people—including me—in the most vicious ways, I had no intention of painting a bullseye on my forehead.

Many of the people who attended his conferences and work-shops, both in the Craft and out, were groupies with little to no critical thought. I suspect most of them were so thoroughly brainwashed over the years that they sided with their persecutor in some perverse iteration of Stockholm Syndrome. In fact, there were two such members, let's call them Patrick and Matt, who really gave me the creeps! You could tell by talking to him, Patrick was a broken man. Much of his speech comprised cheesy slogans that seemed more automated than thoughtful. When asked difficult questions that required reflection, his expression went blank while saying something like, "I'm not there yet."

Matt was just plain scary. He was sharp and alert and enjoyed destabilizing people with sudden loud behavior, which was about the only thing that made him smile. He had a ghastly, vacant stare that said: the lights are on, but somebody else is home! And I'd have no problem believing he could murder someone in cold blood if given a chance.

So why didn't I just walk away? Why allow myself to be subjected to inhumane and abusive treatment? The reasons are many, and they compound.

First, I was brought up in an abusive family environment requiring constant adaptation that became "normal". Whether the environment is good or bad, we simply adapt to it. In the same way that a farmer no longer smells his cow's manure after years of working with them, a child normalizes the dysfunction of their childhood.

Adaptation helps us survive in the short term, but it slowly kills us as adults because now we unconsciously seek those same dysfunctional behaviors in others. Those behaviors are familiar to us, which generates a false sense of comfort and security. Better the devil you know than the devil you don't know.

Second, the mindset of the occultist/New Ager differs greatly from that of a Christian. Unlike the faith-based salvation imparted to us through Scripture, Freemasonry teaches that man is a flawed being in his default state, but by applying the concepts of the Craft to his life, a Mason may achieve perfection through his works. As such, God or godhood is merely a concept, a goal to achieve through discipline and hard work. Trials are for the purpose of our evolution.

Third, the clarity of thought, and the discernment that the mind of Christ offers the Christian, is not to be underestimated; people who have not received Christ into their hearts can believe such absurdities, and I was proof of this. Jesus doesn't force His way into your life, He knocks politely, and if you don't want to let Him in, He won't insist. He loves us enough to respect our choices, even if those choices lead to pain, suffering, and eventual judgement. I had a long way to go before grasping that simple truth, but the cracks had already formed in the dam of these New Age beliefs.

I didn't want to act rashly; while our treatment enraged me, I believed Freemasonry was the best means to reach "enlightenment" and "ascension," even if their methods were questionable.

I skipped a Lodge meeting or two so I could reflect and seriously considered resigning from Freemasonry, thoroughly disenchanted by what had transpired. I drafted a resignation letter, but then I had a conversation with another brother who was initiated at the same time as Franco and me. After discussing the matter with him, he convinced me to wait it out. Denis had already served two consecutive terms as Grand Master, and Pierre, my Worshipful Master and godfather, had been elected to succeed him. This brother, who we'll call Botrax, reasoned that Denis would take a far less active role in the Lodge and I could skip the occasional Prisma conference.

I suspect there were other people discontented with the whole initiation torture adventure because Denis had reeled in his temper and seemed much friendlier and patient with people, at least for the time being. Probably whispers of his behavior were circulating, which affected the attendance of his conferences and workshops, affecting his cash flow. It seems you can only abuse people and take their money for so long before they get upset.

My resignation letter remained undelivered. I kept going for the time being, but I had serious doubts forming in my mind. I looked ahead and would eventually be raised to the rank of Master Mason.

CHAPTER 15
THE THIRD DEGREE

The third degree of Freemasonry, also known as the Master Mason degree, is the main lobby of the Craft. Masons may tell you that the Master Mason degree is the highest degree that can be achieved; in a sense, this is true. Once you've been "raised," an expression used to refer to someone who has undergone the initiation of the third degree, you can become a Lodge Officer, visit other Lodges freely, and become the Worshipful Master of a Lodge; you've technically been raised to the highest level that Blue Lodge Freemasonry offers.

All the order's "secrets" are embedded like wheat kernels in the fabric of the initiation ritual, but you aren't necessarily aware of their full meaning. Allow me to explain… Think of the Entered Apprentice, Fellow Craft, and Master Mason as a three-stepped staircase, with Master Mason being the highest. Depending on the rite a person belongs to, there are degrees numbered higher, but they are not higher in standing. Once you step off that third step toward the fourth, you don't rise higher; you fall back down. The fourth degree, also known as the Secret Master degree in the

Ancient and Accepted Scottish Rite, is a sort of reboot of the Entered Apprentice; the fifth is a revisited Fellow Craft, and so on.

Freemasonry is essentially a three-step staircase that repeats itself—each time, easing back the veil, giving more insight into the order's secrets.

A person could have already been "initiated" to the Master Mason degree without realizing it, even if they've never been a Freemason. What on earth am I talking about, and how could this happen? Through a movie released in the summer of 2009 called "Transformers: Revenge of The Fallen"[1] You may have heard of it or even seen it. While critics lambasted it across the globe for its shallow dialogue, confusing plot, and copious amounts of mayhem and destruction, it was anything but mindless.

It was actually a carefully and deliberately scripted Masonic initiation ritual portrayed by CGI robots. One of the movie's principal "good-guy" characters, a robot named Optimus Prime, is ambushed by three evil robots determined to rend a very important piece of information from him. Each evil robot attacks him, and the third successfully slays him, but the desired information is not obtained and is declared lost.

Later in the movie, Optimus Prime is "raised" from the dead with the help of a "baddie-turned-good-guy" robot, who sacrifices himself to revive Prime. This newly resurrected Optimus, augmented with a new and improved body, takes flight and defeats the antagonist, a robot aptly named The Fallen, who intends to harness the sun (light) and leave the Earth in "darkness" forever.

This is a highly condensed retelling of the Master Mason initiation ritual in which a man named Hiram Abiff or Hiram Abi, said to be the architect of Solomon's temple, is accosted by three ruffians; Fellow Craft construction workers determined to obtain the password and salary of a Master Mason, which they have not earned. The first two ruffians attack Hiram, each delivering a specific wound. The third ruffian kills him, and the secret password is lost. Hiram Abiff is later "resurrected" using the Master Mason's grip, and the three ruffians are put to death.

If what I've just described leaves you feeling anxious, please don't be. Whatever initiation ritual you may have witnessed or taken part in can be undone, but you must read to the end. You need to understand that this is no-holds-barred spiritual warfare, and the evil ones rely heavily on propaganda to paint themselves as the good guys with noble and benevolent objectives.

Freemasons *consider* the Bible one of the recognized Volumes of Sacred Law and claim to use Biblical stories to impart their peculiar form of morality. Still, this is merely a smokescreen. While the Bible mentions Hiram Abiff as a master craftsman (2 Chronicles 2:13-14, NIV), nothing in the Holy Scriptures shows he was murdered. In the Master Mason catechism, we learn of another character named Hiram: the King of Tyre. He is one of the three pillars of Freemasonry, along with Solomon, the King of Israel, and Hiram Abiff, who was killed, according to the Freemasons.

Interestingly, if you look up the etymology of the name Hiram, it has Phoenician origins and can translate to "arrogant" or "pompous." Abiff/Abi means "father," and Freemasons are told that Hiram Abiff is the "father" of the Craft. That said, the word may have an even more sinister meaning. In Hurrian (the language of the Hittites from the Old Testament), the word "Abi" refers to an underground pit the Hittites used to communicate with the underworld and summon their (demonic) deities. In short, it was a portal. I'm sure you see where I'm going with this.

Now let's look at the King of Tyre. This character is mentioned in 1 Kings 5:1-18. On the surface, he seems like a relatively good guy, considering he contributed to the construction of Solomon's temple. However, I suspect the term "King of Tyre" used in Masonic catechism is a double entendre. The name comes up later in the Bible, and while it was used to describe an earthly, mortal man in 2 Chronicles, Ezekiel uses it again, and the passage is less-than-flattering. Ezekiel 28:1-19 (NIV) reads as follows (underline added for emphasis):

A PROPHECY AGAINST THE KING OF TYRE

The word of the Lord came to me: "Son of man, say to the ruler of Tyre, 'This is what the Sovereign Lord says: "'In the pride of your heart you say, "I am a god; I sit on the throne of a god in the heart of the seas." But you are a mere mortal and not a god, though you think you are as wise as a god. Are you wiser than Daniel? Is no secret hidden from you? By your wisdom and understanding you have gained wealth for yourself and amassed gold and silver in your treasuries. By your great skill in trading you have increased your wealth, and because of your wealth your heart has grown proud. "'Therefore this is what the Sovereign Lord says: "'Because you think you are wise, as wise as a god, I am going to bring foreigners against you, the most ruthless of nations; they will draw their swords against your beauty and wisdom and pierce your shining splendor. <u>They will bring you down to the pit, and you will die a violent death</u> in the heart of the seas. Will you then say, "I am a god," in the presence of those who kill you? You will be but a mortal, not a god, in the *hands of those who slay you. You will die the death of the uncircumcised at the hands of foreigners. I have spoken, declares the Sovereign Lord.'" The word of the Lord came to me: "Son of man, take up a lament concerning the king of Tyre and say to him: 'This is what the Sovereign Lord says: "'You were the seal of perfection, full of wisdom and perfect in beauty. <u>You were in Eden</u>, the garden of God; every precious stone adorned you: carnelian, chrysolite and emerald, topaz, onyx and jasper, lapis lazuli, turquoise and beryl. Your settings and mountings were made of gold; on the day you were created they were prepared. <u>You were anointed as a guardian cherub</u>, for so I ordained you. You were on the holy mount of God; you walked among the fiery stones.*

You were blameless in your ways from the day you were created till wickedness was found in you.

Through your widespread trade you <u>were filled with violence, and you sinned.</u> So I drove you in disgrace from the mount of God, and I expelled you, <u>guardian cherub</u>, from among the fiery stones.

Your heart became proud on account of your beauty, and you corrupted your wisdom because of your splendor. So I threw you to the earth; I made a spectacle of you before kings. By your many sins and dishonest trade you have desecrated your sanctuaries. So I made a fire come out from you, and it consumed you, and <u>I reduced you to ashes on the ground in the sight of all who were watching</u>. All the nations who knew you are appalled at you; you have come to a horrible end and will be no more.'"

— EZEKIEL 28:1-19 (NIV), UNDERLINE
ADDED FOR EMPHASIS

Those who are proficient in Scripture recognize the above passage is a parable that parallels the earthly King of Tyre with a corrupt heavenly being; one who sought to place himself above God's throne and, in doing so, was condemned to die like a man. This passage about the King of Tyre is eerily similar to the passage in Isaiah, who compares the King of Babylon to this would-be throne usurper:

> *"Your splendor has been brought down to Sheol, along with the*
> *music of your harps.*
> *Maggots are spread out under you, and worms cover you.* <u>*Shining*</u>
> <u>*morning star,*</u> *how you have fallen from the heavens! You*
> *destroyer of nations,* <u>*you have been cut down to the ground.*</u> *You*
> *said to yourself:* <u>*"I will ascend to the heavens; I will set up my*</u>
> <u>*throne above the stars of God.*</u> *I will sit on the mount of the*
> *gods' assembly, in the remotest parts of the North. I will ascend*
> *above the highest clouds;*
> <u>*I will make myself like the Most High.*</u> *"*

> — ISAIAH 14:11-14 (HCSB), UNDERLINE
> ADDED FOR EMPHASIS

Some might say this passage describes Satan, and it may well be, but there is nothing in Scripture to link this being described by Isaiah or Ezekiel with the nachash (serpent) in the Garden of Eden. In fact, this entity is referred to as the day star or Lucifer in the King James translation. So, who is this King of Tyre if he isn't Satan?

While he *was* expelled from the Garden, Satan was never explicitly stated to have died a violent death in Biblical or non-canonical texts. While he was cast down to the "ground," the Hebrew text could be translated as either Sheol (the realm of the dead) or simply the ground. Now, if we look at what the Apostle Peter has to say about Satan:

Be sober, be vigilant; because your adversary the devil <u>walks about</u> like a roaring lion, seeking whom he may devour.

— 1 PETER 5:8 (NKJV), UNDERLINE ADDED
FOR EMPHASIS)

Satan prowls the earth freely. He even tempted Jesus when He was fasting in the desert, as described in the Gospel of Matthew. So, he couldn't have been cast into the pit and still walk the earth freely because, frankly, that would be like throwing someone in jail and not locking the door. To support my argument, I'll point you to a more obscure text called the book of Jubilees. While this text is not canonical, the incident described appears to support the notion that Satan is free to roam the Earth and gives us an explanation of how it came to be so:

> *And the chief of the spirits, Mastema, came and said: 'YAHWEH, Creator, let some of them remain before me, and let them listen to my voice, and do all that I shall say unto them; for if some of them are not left to me, I shall not be able to execute the power of my will on the sons of men; for these are for corruption and leading astray before my judgment, for great is the wickedness of the sons of men.' And He said: Let the tenth part of them remain before him, and let nine parts descend into the place of condemnation.' And one of us He commanded that we should teach Noah all their medicines; for He knew that they would not walk in uprightness, nor strive in righteousness. And we did according to all His words: all the malignant evil ones we bound in the place of condemnation and a tenth part of them we left that they might be subject before <u>Satan on the earth.</u>*

The Book of Jubilees 10:8-11[2]This excludes Satan as the King of Tyre and Lucifer, but perhaps more interestingly, there's an actual deity referred to as the King of Tyre, called Melqart. The name comes from Melek-qart, "King of the City" (Tyre). This deity was associated with child sacrifice and was revered by other cultures under names such as El, Baal Hammon, Cronus, and Saturn, but ancient Israelites knew him as Moloch.

Doesn't it make you feel all warm and fuzzy inside, knowing that one of the "pillars" of Freemasonry is named after Moloch, the demon-god of child sacrifice? This coincides with the supposedly lost "sacred" name of God that the Freemason discovers upon their initiation to the Royal Arch (13th) degree in the Ancient and Accepted Scottish Rite, which is Jabulon or Yahbulon. This name is actually a composite of three names by which this demonic entity was known in the ancient world:

1. Yah: a name which, while used to refer to God, was also used of Moloch, in the same way that the Canaanites called him El. This coincides with what's written in Ezekiel 28 and Isaiah 14, whereby this entity sought to exalt himself above the throne of God;
2. Bul/Baal/Bel: which comes from Baal Hammon (or Amon) and translates as "Lord of the incense altar";
3. On: this was one name the Egyptians used to refer to the deity known as the primeval sun god. That is to say, the "sun" that preceded the current day star in the heavens. The Egyptians also called him Shemesh.

The worship of this demonic entity is far more common than most people realize; one need only look around. Some symbols that refer to this monster are the black cube; ancient sun wheels—be they Germanic, Aryan, or other—the horned disc, an Egyptian sun disc with wings; and the bull. Whenever you see an advertisement for a certain energy drink whose logo is comprised of two bulls and a sun disc, you'll know what god they venerate.

While this revelation alone should be enough to make your skin crawl, we shouldn't cast Hiram Abiff aside just yet. His true identity and role are far more insidious than the average Master Mason realizes. This brings us back to the movie "Transformers: Revenge of The Fallen" and why Optimus Prime was resurrected in Egypt of all places. If you dig a little deeper into the origins of the Master Mason ritual, it can be traced back as far as ancient Egypt, at least, not the building of Solomon's temple. In fact, when the newly resurrected Optimus Prime takes flight in this movie, he incarnates the ancient Egyptian god Horus, the King of the sky, who is the resurrected form of the dead Osiris.

So how does Horus/Osiris fit into all of this? In the Eastern part of every Masonic Lodge, also called the Orient, placed atop either the Worshipful Master's chair or on the wall behind and above the Worshipful Master's head, is a symbol you've likely seen before. It consists of a triangle with an eye in the center, commonly called the "All-Seeing Eye," which represents the Grand Architect of The Universe, the god of the Freemasons. This symbol also comes from ancient Egypt, but they call it by a different name: the Eye of Osiris/Horus.

Some scholars postulate that the story of Osiris/Horus precedes ancient Egypt, that its origins and characters can be traced back to ancient Uruk, and while the names of characters and deities were changed, the essence of the story was preserved. To the Mesopotamians, Horus was Ninurta, and to the Akkadians, he was Sargon. The ancient Hebrews called him Nimrod.

If we look closely at Genesis 10, verses 8 and 9 (NIV), we read that: Cush was the father of Nimrod, who became a mighty warrior on the Earth. He was a mighty hunter before the Lord;

that is why it is said, "Like Nimrod, a mighty hunter before the Lord."

We can also look to the Benson Commentary on Biblehub.com [3]for additional insight into these passages: "It is probable he began with hunting, and for this became famous to a proverb. He served his country by ridding it of wild beasts, and so insinuating himself into the affections of his neighbors, he became their prince. And perhaps, under the pretense of hunting, he gathered men under his command to make himself master of the country. Thus, he became a mighty hunter, *a violent invader of his neighbors' rights and properties*." (italics added for emphasis)

In short, Nimrod was a tyrant, a dictator, and the all-seeing eye that the Freemasons call the Grand Architect of The Universe is the fallen god he worshipped. It is also the symbol used on the United States' one-dollar bill. The structure below the eye looks a bit like an Egyptian pyramid, but I believe it more aptly represents the tower of Babel, which is now understood by most scholars to have been a ziggurat.

Nimrod was the one who re-ignited the dark flame of the cult of Shemjaza (A.K.A. Osiris, Moloch, Dagon, Saturn, El, Enlil) upon the earth, which I believe is how he became a "mighty man," and also why Moloch and Nimrod are often associated with one another. In ancient cultures, this fallen god was the primeval sun, or the black sun, the sun that shone before the current sun. I believe he is the one named Apollyon in the book of Revelation, the one who will be released from the pit during the Final Tribulation.

While there is no smoking gun, there comes a preponderance of damning evidence in all the little details of the names, symbols, and rituals the Freemasons employ and the characters the Freemasons venerate.

While I prefer sparing you this rather extensive rabbit trail from my testimony, I felt it was necessary to give you a rudimentary overview of how everything interconnects. Providing you with just my testimony risks leaving you with more questions than answers. I thought it wiser to intermingle this understanding, which came to me much later, hoping to make my story more comprehensible.

Alas, this is what I was involved in, and while I had fleeting glimpses of insight here and there, it wasn't enough to paint a clear picture for me at the time.

For the Master Mason initiation ritual and all subsequent "Middle Chamber" meetings, the Lodge configuration remained the same from the two previous degrees, but they replaced the red tablecloths with black ones. I'd also like to take this opportunity to point out another interesting little detail about the Lodge; it seems to fit in with all the other bothersome details I've already pointed out for you. We were told that the layout of a Masonic Lodge is based on the Biblical plans of Solomon's Temple, because it is twice as long as it is wide; has two bronze columns at the entrance, one called Jakin and the other Boaz; and the opposite end of the entrance, where the Worshipful Master sits, represents the Holy of Holies.

There is, however, one major discrepancy—let's set aside the fact that the Worshipful Master sits in the Most Holy place, pretending to be God—Solomon's temple was oriented such that the Holy of Holies was in the West and the entrance with the columns was in the East. A Masonic Temple is inverted, with the entrance in the West and the Holy of Holies in the East. This brings to mind the passage in Ezekiel, where God takes him and shows him the abominations taking place in the temple; namely that the people have turned their backs on the Lord, choosing instead to venerate strange gods:

> *Then He brought me into the inner courtyard of the Lord's house. And behold, at the entrance to the temple of the LORD, between the porch and the altar, were about twenty-five men <u>with</u> their backs to the temple of the LORD while <u>their faces were toward the east</u>; and they were prostrating themselves eastward toward the sun.*
>
> — EZEKIEL 8:16 (NASB), UNDERLINE ADDED
> FOR EMPHASIS

Those who have been in the Craft for any length of time will tell you that as you rise in degrees, your schedule fills up quickly. Besides the Blue and White Lodge meetings, you also have Fellow Craft Lodge meetings and now Master Mason Lodge meetings, known as the Middle Chamber. Add three initiations per year, one for each degree of the Blue Lodge, and of course, you still must provide the three minimum pieces of architecture per year. Things can quickly get busy. I suspect this is all by design.

They aim to keep your nose to the grindstone, keeping you focused on the material they give you, learning all the symbols, dialogue, and signs. If one were to step back and take the time to probe deeper into the meaning of things, they might see what the higher-ups don't want them to see. At least, not just yet.

At first, it was manageable, but little by little, my solicitation increased. Initially, a mere spectator at initiations, I was now asked to assist, if only in minor ways. I was also asked to take over the role of organizing the banquets for Zenith Lodge number two. Franco had initially accepted the position, besides taking a position as a Junior Warden but found his schedule too full, and after just a few months, asked me to take over for him.

It's fascinating how much your view of people can change with time. While my initial impression of Masons was that they were generous and helpful people, that veneer slipped away. For one, getting people to take part in the banquets—bring a dish—was like pulling teeth. I often ended up preparing a few dishes to bring, just so we could have a proper banquet. Usually, people stayed for the banquet long enough to have a bite, then run out the door, leaving a handful of us to wash all the dishes, put the food away, clean the tables, pick up the empty cups, sweep the floor, and take out the trash. I ended up being the last one to lock up for the night more often than not.

As part of our Lodge Officer appointments, they promoted Sylvain from Junior to Senior Warden of our Lodge. The tiny spider fissures in the facade of Freemasonry were about to grow into visible cracks!

CHAPTER 16
TWO TYPES OF PEOPLE

Something my former godfather Pierre, the Grand Master, once told me etched itself into my brain. He said if you want to see what someone is really like, give them power. I believe this was one of those times when God slipped His way into the mouth of a heathen and inspired him to utter a prophetic truth to herald his undoing.

In my limited experience, there are two types of Freemasons. The first is well-intentioned but lost and searching for answers; this group makes up what I call "the outer circle" and is the hard-working but not astute people Freemasonry loves to use for public relations. They make up the majority of members; they're always volunteering and offering to help. Many times, they carry the bulk of the workload in the Lodge.

Then there's the other type of Freemason, what I call "the social climber." These are the ones who are very ambitious by nature but never really achieve anything significant in their everyday lives, and they view Freemasonry as a means to their own self-aggrandizement. They're just itching to be in a position of authority, and when they get it, the little power they have goes to their head, and eventually, they derail. Denis, Pierre, Franco, and Sylvain all fall into this category. Most Lodges comprise about thirty people, including the Officers, so it's usually not too long before you're appointed to an officer's position or delegated certain responsibilities.

Sylvain, for example, had quite a checkered past. Besides various financial projects he'd been involved in, some legit and some not-so-legit, he had also been a "conspiracy theory" speaker, lecturing on and promulgating flowcharts of the elite hierarchy. Not based on first-hand experience or facts, mind you, just rumors and things he'd read or found on the internet. His lectures were surprisingly anti-Masonic, at least until Denis recruited him. Sylvain previously shared that he initially joined Freemasonry intending to expose them from the inside out. They saw him coming from a mile away and figured him out rather quickly.

Sylvain was insecure; he craved attention, prestige, and power, just like Denis and Franco; nobodies who wanted to be big shots with a commanding presence and eager to take every shortcut to get it. The most significant difference was that Denis was considerably more cunning than either of them and instrumentally manipulated Sylvain, Franco, and Pierre into a convoluted business scheme that exploded in their respective faces and dealt a blow to the Grand Lodge of Canada. God knows precisely how to flip the tables on evil people and use their twisted schemes to sink them—but not yet.

Sylvain embarked upon a new business venture, and things looked very promising. He reaped the initial fruits of success, and it showed. It's late winter of 2014, and I was off to attend a W. L. meeting that closely followed on the heels of a freakish snowstorm that Southern Quebec is notorious for. Upon arriving at the Lodge, clearly some Officers wouldn't be able to attend, and wouldn't you know it, one of the other Officers urged me to serve as a replacement.

I was uneasy at the prospect. Our Lodge prided itself on its officers' quality and the rigor with which they performed the opening and closing rituals. Unless you've ever witnessed or participated in it, you couldn't understand how technical it can be, especially when you have to simultaneously play more than one role. I didn't want to do it!

After considerable prodding from the other Officer, I reluctantly agreed, and Sylvain and another brother were having the time of their lives watching me sweat. In fact, they spent much of the opening ritual poking fun at me and trying to trip me up. That's another trait of insecure people; they relish any opportunity to put others down to make themselves feel better. Sylvain and Franco were on an upswing, and their egos were ballooning, much to the ire of their fellow brothers and sisters.

I occasionally served as a replacement Officer in the Lodge in various positions, namely as Chaplain, Master of Ceremony, Tyler, and Almoner. Of these Officer positions, the Tyler was the most interesting and simultaneously the least important. As the Lodge security guard, my job was to stand at the door of the Lodge, sword in hand, and make sure no one interrupted the proceedings. I ensured those in attendance were duly qualified by engaging each member in a discreet series of questions and answers to test their Masonic proficiency as they entered the Lodge.

Once I'd played the roles and became accustomed to them, it became much easier. Still, something within me dreaded the idea of being a full-time Officer. Despite that, Pierre and several others were quite surprised, if not mildly impressed, by how well I performed in those duties, despite my discomfort. They were all eager and itching for me to "volunteer" as a formal Officer of the Lodge, but deep down, it felt like something dark and creepy was longing to sink its claws into me.

The situation with my father was becoming strained again; just as before, he tried to start pointless arguments or provoke me. My workload and the increasing demands of the Lodge began wearing me down. I was becoming snappy and irritable.

As if that wasn't bad enough, in November of that year, both my parents landed in the hospital at the same time for cardiac conditions. I played nursemaid to my temporarily disabled parents, besides everything else. I was burning the candle at both ends, and the forces of darkness were slowly turning the screws on me, intent on breaking me yet again. The strain was showing.

Never missing a trick, Sylvain, along with Pierre, used our next meeting as an opportunity to gently but publicly "scold" me for allowing myself to destabilize because of the recent events. It's simply unbecoming for a Master Mason to be taken aback by events; we must model exemplary behavior for the lower-downs—stiff upper lip, etc.

Sylvain took perverse pleasure in watching others suffer, perhaps more than anyone else. Whether by playing cruel practical jokes on them or using his position of authority to scold people for what he perceived to be their failings, he relished the opportunity to make them feel small in his presence. Another attribute common to insecure people is jealousy, and what's peculiar is that it's not even aimed at the people they're competing with. I wanted nothing that Sylvain had.

I never sought attention, power, or position within the Lodge. Neither did I want to get even for all the practical jokes he played or the times he tried to exert dominance over me. Sylvain was a sad, petty little man. Not that he was actually little; at six feet four inches, he was a tall and hefty fellow, hardly someone you'd think would have self-esteem issues. Insecurity is like a black hole that knows neither creed nor color; no matter how much money, popularity, lovers, or shiny bobbles you pour into it, you never feel whole.

By the spring of 2015, I attained the rank of Secret Master. New regalia; new password; new gestures; and a new, more chilling oath. While I had dunked my little toe into the waters of the Lodge of Perfection—the degrees from 4 to 14—my enthusiasm waned. The secrecy and novelty of the Craft had lost their luster, and I was just plain tired. While I was doing reasonably well in my career as a model maker, I felt stuck in a rut, almost like I was missing my calling; I felt unsatisfied, and I needed a change. The familiar things that previously brought me comfort now felt stuffy and in my way. I didn't know it then, but this marked the start of the countdown of my final year in the Craft.

Also, during this time, Sylvain's business in the credit industry was burgeoning, and Franco was enjoying the fruits of a new job in the computer sector. You'd think that someone earning a low six-figure salary would be more comfortable financially, but Franco came to me, asking for a personal loan. You might think it was a mistake for me to oblige him. In hindsight, I agree, but I got something in return; I saw how irresponsible and utterly shameless he was. Furthermore, I was tired of constantly chasing my Lodge members, to get them to take part in the banquets, and dealing with last-minute cancelations. I wasn't the only one whose motivation was on the wane.

To make matters worse, I'd quarreled with my father just days before and injured my back while helping him lift something far too heavy. By early summer, the weight of all these burdens finally took its toll on me, and I suffered another nervous breakdown.

CHAPTER 17
THE BREAKING POINT

The situation was serious. People aren't supposed to have nervous breakdowns this easily. Was I just feeble? Even daily tasks seemed like mountains, and I had lost the motivation for the simplest pleasures in life. Part of me desperately wanted help, and the other was too exhausted. I could no longer concentrate, and my sleep came in spurts. I needed help but didn't know where to turn or whom to ask.

I'd had some abysmal experiences with government healthcare workers years back when my then-girlfriend had gone through difficult times. Having vowed not to repeat the same mistake, I searched for alternative solutions. After some tedious internet research, I found a private talk therapist and promptly made an appointment. I was exhausted, but I also knew things would worsen if I didn't get help right then.

The therapist was diplomatic but also candid. I asked her to be as direct with me as possible under the circumstances, and she didn't disappoint! It's amazing how bad things needed to get before it shook me out of my stupor. But there I was, broken, exhausted, and forced to confront the painful reality that I had been at least partially responsible for letting things get to this point.

Within a few sessions, I realized how I'd been conditioned to appease my parents as a child and how this conditioning had spilled over into my adult life. I was taking everyone else's problems onto my shoulders, and eventually, my mind collapsed under the strain of it all.

The summer months were put to good use, reading psychology books and getting some much-needed rest. The therapy sessions led me to revisit many long-held beliefs and habits and examine the nature of my relationships. I would have to put my foot down and make changes that would benefit me, and if people didn't like it, that would be their problem.

The Lodge and Freemasonry were on the chopping block but wouldn't leave quietly. Since Freemasons, particularly high-ranking Masons, work with demons, those entities picked up on what was happening and conveyed this back to Pierre, Denis, and Maryse. Unbeknownst to me, they were already hatching a plan to hold on to me.

As things started looking up in August, they asked me to attend an informal Masonic get-together at Sylvain's house. Some new candidates for the Lodge were in attendance, and Pierre thought it would be a good idea to have a sit-down and answer some questions they might have. But Sylvain and Pierre had another reason for inviting me.

Sylvain's enterprise, now called the Canadian Credit Corporation, hereafter CCC, expanded during this time. He hired Pierre, appointed him C.E.O., and hired Denis as a "Consultant." I should note that neither of these men had any competencies or experience for these positions, but we'll come back to that.

I didn't find out until much later that Sylvain's business partner, a man we shall call Robert, a newly initiated E. A. himself, recently made an acrimonious break with the firm, taking a significant portion of the funding with him. Desperate to save his sinking ship, Sylvain had to act quickly; they needed an urgent influx of capital to keep their Titanic afloat. Rather than turn to private investors or a bank, which would take too long, they concocted a plan to recruit, train and hire a dozen people to work as credit analysts. However, since this type of industry was still new, there were no training resources available. Sylvain created a training program and offered it to applicants for a modest sum of $5,500 per person.

During that get-together, Pierre took me aside and asked me to take a walk with him just as things were winding down. When we were alone on the road, he told me he would channel a message from an entity destined for me. Pierre's face and demeanor suddenly changed, and he or this demon began telling me I was failing my life's mission. He claimed the work I was doing was the opposite of what the Grand Architect of the Universe intended for me. If I didn't act quickly to rectify the situation, many years of suffering would be in store for me.

I was just starting to get things under control, and this came along and utterly crushed me. The demons knew I was vulnerable; they picked their opportunity and jammed the knife into my proverbial ribs with everything they had. The look on my face said it all: I felt like my life was a complete train wreck, and that's precisely what Pierre and Sylvain wanted to hear. Naturally, they extended a hand of friendship now that they thoroughly beat me down and offered a "brother" a new job opportunity at the modest price tag of $5,500.

Feeling trapped and discouraged by the revelation I'd just heard, compounded by the questionable state of mind I was already in, I accepted the offer. Because my mental health had taken a toll on my work, finances were tight, and I'd already withdrawn from my savings to make ends meet. The cost of the course I had enrolled in compounded this. The forces of darkness had played me like a grand piano, steering me directly where they wanted me to go, right back into the waiting arms of the Lodge conspirators.

What was peculiar about Sylvain's new credit enterprise was that all but three of his hires were fellow Freemasons. Even the landlord he rented from was a fellow Mason from a neighboring Lodge. While I was initially puzzled why Sylvain would name Pierre—a man with absolutely no business experience—as C.E.O. of the firm, I quickly came to learn why. During one of our meetings, I was allowed to overhear a conversation between Pierre, Sylvain, and some other Lodge members. Because of Sylvain's colorful past, they deemed this would taint the enterprise's credibility.

Moreover, Sylvain's ex-business partner, Robert, a very business-savvy and adept man, would likely expose what he'd just experienced to the public. They needed someone with a better public image, like a retired police officer, a man who knew the ins and outs of the legal system. This man "handled" anyone sniffing around the enterprise, hoping to expose inconvenient truths. It didn't matter that Pierre had no business experience. They needed a watchdog, more than anything else, to appease their enemies while simultaneously looking respectable enough to the financial firms they were courting.

If you already think these people were of questionable moral character, allow me to share what I confirmed after piecing together why Sylvain and Robert split so acrimoniously. While I've already established that Denis, Past Grand Master of the Grand Lodge of Canada and President of Prisma, was a narcissist and a bully, he had yet another dirty secret. Denis was a compulsive fornicator—young, old, married, single; it didn't matter to him. He had slept with many married female Masons, even though he was publicly dating someone who was, herself, a Mason and an Officer of the Grand Lodge. At the same time, he was extremely cautious about preserving his public image. He also delighted in taking explicit photographs of his sexual conquests, which he stored on his home computer.

Denis had made a move on Robert's girlfriend. Furious and disgusted with the behavior of his would-be mentor, Robert promptly split and dissociated himself from Sylvain, his business, and everything to do with the Lodge.

Remember what I said previously about there being no honor among thieves?

While I didn't know it yet, the events I described above turned out to be a major fracture in the dam of the Grand Lodge of Canada. While I still didn't have the complete picture, I was making out a vague image from the puzzle pieces, and I didn't like what I saw. In addition, voices of discontent arose within the Grand Lodge. Fellow brothers and sisters were becoming disgusted with the arrogance, narcissism, and two-faced behaviors of Franco, Sylvain, and Denis. One of the most ardent voices of dissent came from a fellow Mason who was also Sylvain's childhood friend.

I was angry and resentful, and I also felt trapped because I was strapped financially and already committed to the credit analyst course. I want to clarify one crucial point: a business mantra had practically been driven into us from the beginning of our training. *Our job is to accurately reflect the truth of a customer's credit report.*

Things were already shifting within the CCC. Everyone who signed up for the analyst course did so with Sylvain's assurance that the job only comprised analyzing clients' credit records and updating them. Sylvain was to provide us with said clients. But of course, like any used-car salesman, Sylvain was adept at changing the rules, so he did.

Upon graduating from the class, we were displeased to find that clients weren't lined-up and waiting for us to graduate as we'd been told. In fact, it was all quite dead and quiet in early December 2015 when many former students, myself included, started thinking we'd been had. So, what did Sylvain do? He urged us to pick up telephone directories and begin cold-calling financial institutions to promote our services to them. Many of us were upset at hearing this, but Christmas was just around the corner, and budgets were tight. We needed customers and income, so most of us grudgingly accepted.

I should point out that I hadn't had a chance to fully recover from my breakdown due to all these rapidly unfolding events from last summer. I went from the frying pan into the fire. My adrenals were exhausted, and my stress tolerance was low. To top it all off, I was asked to cold-call people to drum up business, something I utterly loathe, pushing my stress levels over the edge.

In the days leading up to Christmas, a member of our team finally snagged a client. We decided it would be an excellent exercise to review the client's credit report as a team under Sylvain's direct supervision. It was to no surprise when we found several corrections to make. One glaring error, when corrected, caused the client's credit score to go down, not up. And what did Sylvain instruct us to do on our very first credit assignment? "Leave it alone," he said, "if the client's score goes down, they might ask for a refund!"

So much for *"our job is to accurately reflect the truth of a customer's credit report."*

One of the non-Masonic people who had taken the course with us, who we'll call Sylvie, confided in me about how utterly bizarre she thought many of the people at the CCC were. She told me they used identical phrases and expressions in an almost mindless and robotic fashion—like they were all in the same cult! I don't think she brought this to my attention by chance; sometimes, the Lord will find an unmistakable and unexpected way to bring a message right to our ears. I heard this one as clear as a bell! *Thank you, Lord; your servant is listening.*

Sylvie was terminated shortly after this happened for criticizing the unprofessional and improvised way the CCC was being run. While that was bad enough, what happened next came as a shock to me and several other disgruntled colleagues. We had all received a memo in our software interface program from Pierre, proclaiming Sylvie's departure from the CCC. He depicted how utterly negligent and unprofessional her conduct had been in administrating her duties; a communique that was libelous! Pierre, seeming to realize what he'd done and deleted the message. Thankfully, one analyst had taken a screen capture before it was deleted and shared it with the people who had already left.

I contacted Sylvie privately after her dismissal to see how she was doing. Despite having the libelous email image, she determined that pursuing legal remedy was more trouble than it was worth, and she preferred to look ahead to better things.

I was done. Not only was I thoroughly disgusted with the CCC and its members, but over the holidays, I'd experienced a serious malfunction with a piece of computer hardware. That simple, little straw was the one that broke the camel's back; I broke down and sobbed uncontrollably.

When I showed up at the main office on January 4th, 2016, it was only to gather my things and tell them I wouldn't be coming back. The depleted look on my face matched the expressions of surprise from the team and Sylvain. He knew he was the first mate of a sinking ship.

CHAPTER 18
THE TELL ALL

Upon leaving the office, I headed straight for the medical clinic. I was in bad shape, and this was the only sensible thing I could think of. I must've looked horrible because they let me see a doctor right away, which is unheard of in Quebec. There was no hiding the fact that I was distraught. After answering several questions, the doctor ordered a series of tests, and a psychological evaluation, to which I gladly agreed. If I was mentally ill, I needed to know.

I spent several weeks alone, mulling over everything I'd gone through in the last few years, questioning my choices, and re-evaluating the people I thought were my friends. I had called to cancel several Lodge meetings and even skipped a Secret Master initiation. Unbeknownst to me, other Masons noticed my absence and were talking. I had been a very active member of the Lodge, frequently volunteering and offering help and guidance to my fellow Masons and keeping them well-fed. I was a good PR man for the Craft, and suddenly I wasn't around anymore.

It's incredible how moochers only really notice how much they depend on you when you're not available for them to mooch on anymore.

I stayed in contact with several ex-CCC students during this time. One of them confided to me that Pierre had tried to get him to back-date and sign a revised version of the contract we had all signed in early September of the previous year. Sylvain and Pierre were undoubtedly getting nervous and fearing legal reprisals for the sham they were involved in. They were desperately trying to cover their tracks.

I had to give my Masonic career a serious evaluation. Despite all the bad things I'd seen and experienced, I'd held on this long because I thought it was the best road to enlightenment. Clearly, that illusion was now shattered. People like Pierre, Denis, and Maryse had all gone to the very top, and what did they have to show for it? They were deceitful, manipulative, narcissistic, power-hungry, abusive, and vain with raging egos. Either Freemasonry wasn't doing its job—rendering it worthless—or it *was* doing its job, and the results were proving worthless. Regardless of which was true, I no longer wanted any part of it.

In mid-March, I showed up at the Lodge for the last time. Several colleagues were both happy and surprised to see me when I arrived early to gather my things. They were eager to speak with me about Masonic subjects, but I wasn't having any of it. I was simply there to drop off my last piece of architecture and leave. There was a mixture of surprise and worry in their expressions when I walked out before the meeting. I can't express how much lighter I felt when I walked out of the temple and out of that building, knowing I'd never set foot in there again.

You must be wondering why they just allowed me to leave. Weren't they going to threaten or harass me? Wasn't there a chance they would try to eliminate me? And why did I drop off a piece of architecture? That's the thing with Freemasonry: they make you jump through hoops to get into the Craft, but the door is open should you decide to leave.

Interestingly, quite a few people had left over the almost five years of my Masonic career. At first, it was customary for an officer or fellow Mason to read the departed person's resignation letter before the Lodge. That custom quickly ended because you can't have disgruntled ex-members revealing some of the disgusting and reprehensible things they'd seen, heard, or experienced to the other Lodge members; it might reveal some dirty secrets and cause more people to walk out in droves.

As for the last piece of architecture I mentioned earlier, that was my resignation letter. Ever since Pierre had pulled the demonic revelation card on me months earlier, I had done some research. Now that I'd been on the "inside" of the Craft for some time, I had a better understanding and could more justly parse the information I found, and some of it made my stomach turn.

The history of Freemasonry is one of scandal, treachery, murder, infiltration, and a host of grotesque crimes. One of the more recent scandals involved a famous British celebrity named Jimmy Savile. Shortly after his death, they discovered he had been a rampant pedophile and necrophiliac for several decades. Yes, Jimmy Savile, the same one awarded the order of the British Empire and knighted by Pope John Paul II. Pro-tip: any time you hear of anyone being knighted, it's because they're part of an occult order. They do not give such titles to the profane, common everyday people who haven't taken a blood-curdling oath to some secret society.

If that weren't bad enough, they later revealed that Freemasons helped cover up his crimes. These were just some of the disgusting facts I discovered about the Craft, and I called the Grand Lodge and Lodge members out—in writing. I called them a bunch of vampires that preyed on the public at large and their own members. I told them they needed to examine their consciences, their professed values, and how they measured up to their actions. I was polite but direct.

It did not surprise me that this piece of architecture wasn't circulated within the Lodge, but fellow Lodge members were curious about what happened. Some called me, and I not only explained the situation, I sent them a copy of my letter. Something they could chew on, digest, and share. It was an understatement to say that they were taken aback by what they read. Many later confided that they also had experienced and seen some rather disturbing things.

My paper eventually reached Franco, who was also shocked by its contents. He called me, and we discussed the events. Of course, he denied any wrongdoing, but he shared an important piece of information: he had been aware of Denis' infidelity for some time. While installing software updates on Denis' computer, he saw graphic pictures of the women Denis had seduced, but he kept quiet about it. He also confessed that shortly after the business break-up Sylvain had with Robert, Pierre enlisted him to hack Robert's private computer to find and delete any information that Robert had gathered against them that could be used as leverage or incriminating evidence.

Why hadn't he come clean about these things sooner? That's the thing with vampires: they see everything in the mirror except themselves. Franco didn't think it was a problem that Denis was sleeping-around because he had done it too, as had Sylvain. In retrospect, it's no surprise they were so close, always hanging out together. Deep down, they were all the same and had similar dysfunctions. They could not see their own behaviors as evil, so they projected their flaws onto other people, condemning them. Their vanity and pride choked out their capacity for self-reflection. However cruel and abusive they'd been with me, the mental prison they constructed for themselves was a far worse fate. Little did I know, their ordeal was far from over.

Sylvain and Pierre were notoriously quiet. Sylvain often laid low when confronted with something that jarred his conscience, as was his custom. For all his attempts at self-aggrandizement, he had a poor poker face. The remorseful puppy-dog eyes were unmistakable whenever he was caught with his hand in the proverbial cookie jar. I wasn't expecting much of a response either way, but I felt like something was coming—something big!

CHAPTER 19
SKELETON EXPOSE

Things remained quiet for about two months. Seemingly out of the blue, Franco called me, saying we really needed to talk. He seemed agitated—more so than usual. The piece of architecture I'd circulated had rattled some cages and troubled some consciences. Both Sylvain and Pierre did some digging, and what they found was jaw-dropping!

Our dear past Grand Master, and Sovereign Grand Inspector General, Denis, was a fraud! All his prestigious contacts, international rendezvous with high-level Masons, his fabled pedigree, all his glorious titles, the certificate given to him by Pope John Paul II; all lies! Denis was not initiated into Freemasonry at 18 years of age by his illustrious father, as we were told, but in his middle age in 2001. Sylvain ran into someone from Denis's past, the man who initiated him.

Worse yet, they kicked Denis out of the order in 2003 for the same nonsense he was still doing in the Grand Lodge of Canada. As if that wasn't bad enough, he had pressured his Worshipful Master at the time to initiate him to the 33rd degree by the alleged order of Pope John Paul II. Denis agreed to "pay" for that initiation, promising his Worshipful Master the sum of $8,650, of which he only delivered $3,100. But wait, there's more!

The Grand Lodge of Canada wasn't founded in 1982, as we were told. Denis had been rummaging through the articles of a yard sale one fine day and found the patent letters for the Lodge among the effects of a deceased Mason, someone he never even knew. It had been in slumber for some time. He had acquired the paperwork for a song and dance and just began operating.

All the pseudo-Masonic formations Denis offered through Prisma with the assurance that they were recognized internationally had no such accreditation; all the diplomas he awarded people weren't worth the paper they were printed on.

Also, while at the Grand Lodge of Canada, Denis and Maryse were in charge of the books and, while operating predominantly with cash, had absconded with over eighty thousand dollars of the Grand Lodge's funds. Worse, Prisma volunteers were the ones who brought the significant irregularities in their books to our attention. As a non-profit organization, there were books to be balanced and people to answer to; failing to do either would lead to serious legal ramifications.

Remember what I said about there being no honor among thieves? Of all the people who were shocked and devastated by these discoveries, I think it hit Pierre the hardest. Having been a police officer in his younger years, a man who prided himself on his investigative skills, he never saw this coming. Sylvain much later confirmed that when the stream of resignations began coming in, mine included, they started digging. When the evidence of Denis' first removal from the order was discovered, Pierre broke down and sobbed.

Pierre had been a career Mason for well over two decades, traveled to many Lodges, and met countless other Masons. Despite his much-touted skills as an investigator, he had allowed a fraudster, with a fraction of his Masonic experience, to be his mentor, godfather, and confidant. He let the guy in, right under his nose, and suspected nothing.

The following verses from the book of Proverbs come to mind when reflecting on the situation:

> *Pride goes before destruction, and a haughty spirit before a fall.*

> — PROVERBS 16:18 (ESV)

> *Everyone who is arrogant in heart is an abomination to the Lord; be assured, he will not go unpunished.*

> — PROVERBS 16:5 (ESV)

Remember that row Denis had with CLIPSAS board member Elie? During Denis' brief, original tenure as a Mason, he went on an overseas trip with Elie. While abroad, they met a woman whom Denis sexually assaulted. As a result, Elie vowed to have him stricken from the order. The Masonic investigation into Denis' conduct ended with his first removal.

I suppose you're wondering why the sexual assault charge was never mentioned during his first striking. Elie himself may have been implicated, and if he'd pulled too hard on that thread, he'd risk unraveling the whole garment and himself along with it, but I can't confirm that information. It's always a delicate dance with the Freemasons. It's like the mob: they're all bad, but the louder, flashier, and more brazenly corrupt members will invariably bring the heat down on the entire organization. Such people must be eliminated in the most surgical of ways to avoid even more damage. The dark side always consumes its own.

At the Grand Lodge meeting in June of 2016, after a thorough investigation, it was decided to strike both Denis and Maryse from the order for a second time, but it was too little too late. As reported to me later, less than half of the over one hundred members had shown up. All the other people quit! All the devious, dishonest, malicious, and perverse works of evil had finally exploded in their faces; the Grand Lodge of Canada was in tatters.

God takes what the enemy means for evil and turns it for good. Part of me felt vindicated, but I also understood what was happening. It was all too predictable. Denis and Maryse were only part of the problem; though perhaps slightly less guilty, the other members had merely made them scapegoats. The vipers would sacrifice the most rotten among them to save the nest. Still, part of me couldn't help but breathe a sigh of relief.

While I was slowly re-acclimating to normal life, all was not perfect. The dark forces that had tried so desperately to ensnare me were dealt a knock-down blow, but they weren't out. They might have had to regroup, but they were around long before I immersed myself in the occult, and it would only be a matter of time until they took another swing at me. The pinpoints of light I'd become accustomed to seeing were still present, and there was other paranormal activity.

Occasionally, while in light sleep. I felt someone (or something) tugging at my bedsheets; other times, I could feel the mattress around me being depressed, as though someone was on the bed with me.

I had a touch-activated lamp in my living room, right next to the hallway. Sometimes, I walked by, and the light turned itself on; other times, I'd be at my computer at the complete opposite end of the living room, and the lamp would turn itself on. They were letting me know they were still around.

I was also having problems with my kitchen sink drain. Sometimes dirty water would flow back up into my sink, harkening back to the dreams I'd had years before. God was trying to tell me that there was still a major "clog" in my life that needed serious repairing.

Around this time, I received the results of my psychological evaluation. The wait had been long, but after scheduling an appointment for a sit-down, the verdict was in: I wasn't crazy! Besides the results of the tests they'd run on me, the symptoms I'd manifested showed that I'd been under stress for far too long. I could proudly boast of my sanity now, but that left me with more questions than answers. Why had I broken down so easily? What was I not getting? What was behind all the bizarre phenomena? I still wasn't making the connection about the demons, at least not yet.

For the rest of 2016, I continued to live off what remained of my savings, preferring to spend my time researching the occult. I was accumulating data, but connecting the dots was a ways off. Besides everything else, my physical health was suffering. While I'd craved sweets and junk food since childhood, food bingeing was becoming more regular and more extreme; now driven by anxiety about my dwindling finances. Having ballooned to almost 240 lbs., I experienced numbness in my fingers, energy bursts followed by deep crashes, and skin tags beginning to appear, all signs of early-onset diabetes.

The situation with my kitchen sink was getting worse, which compounded my anxiety. In early 2017, the sink issue became unmanageable, so I called a plumber who snaked my drain. Upon retrieving the snake, the plumber pulled out what looked like yellow fiberglass wool; somewhere along the line, the pipe had ruptured—this was serious.

My father was the landlord of the building I lived in, and true to his ways, he was very "repair-averse," fearing the costs that such a repair could entail. The whole situation irritated him, and to deny the magnitude of the damage, he snaked my drain at least twice hoping to alleviate the situation. Despite the dirty water continuously backing up into my sink, he staunchly refused to accept the need for major repairs. When I insisted, he became snappy.

He eventually relented. While that was a minor victory, it meant that my apartment would be a stress-inducing construction zone for at least the next two months.

It wasn't so much that plumbers and construction workers would be around; I could handle that. The problem was that my father was (and remains) an unbridled control freak, determined to micromanage everything the contractors were appointed to do. Despite having zero credentials and only marginal experience doing odd jobs, he felt that because he was paying, he had the authority to tell everyone how to do their jobs, whether rightly or wrongly.

This both annoyed the workers and irritated him. Worst of all, he was in my hair for hours every single day. When he finished annoying the contractors, he hovered around me, trying to provoke a quarrel or badger me into helping him do things the workers were supposed to do. As much as I tried telling him in a kind, calm fashion that they and I didn't need his help, that just made him angrier.

Sometimes I swallowed my words and diffused the situation, but other times my nerves were so frayed that I snapped back. He was like a toddler in an old man's body, and more often than not, he was unreasonable.

The situation eventually escalated to where one day he was in an especially foul mood and was badgering me to do something I didn't want to do. I don't recall the words I uttered that set him off, but he exploded on me. He told me he didn't want me as a tenant anymore and that I should leave.

Something inside me broke. I had cracked under pressure several times before, but this felt different, almost like I had crossed the point of no return. Despair came over me as never before. I felt desolate, like my life was a futile series of failures punctuated with suffering. I wanted to die, but not in the "my life sucks" temporary way; I wanted to end my life, and I knew exactly how to do it!

CHAPTER 20
LIFE OR DEATH

Every problem in my life felt magnified and flooded my mind; each setback I'd experienced in business, every failed relationship, my unhappy childhood. Now, my apartment was in shambles, my savings were depleted, and I was about to be evicted. I'd end up on the street; whatever shades of gray my thoughts had been, they were now black.

It's a curious, surreal, and terrifying feeling to be in the pit of despair; you feel separated from everyone, and everything, and nothing matters anymore. I didn't care whom I'd hurt by ending my own life; I was consumed with grief, despair, and rage and relished the idea of my father suffering the loss of his only son—a cruel, vindictive payback for all the anguish and suffering he'd caused my siblings and me throughout our lives.

I didn't realize that demons were orchestrating this entire drama. My family was already plagued with them, even before I stumbled into the occult. Now that I had joined the ranks of their earthly stooges, I was a promising asset—one of theirs. They don't take kindly to anyone disrupting the ranks, making a mess, and simply walking away, especially one of their own. If I couldn't be brought back into the fold, they would do everything in their power to keep me from joining the light, even if it meant killing me.

I believe demons had a hand in what was happening, but this doesn't mean they had total control or that it absolved me of responsibility for the bad choices I'd made. You don't get to stand before God, point at Satan, and exclaim, "He made me do it!" We always have a choice in what we do, say, and even think. I do, however, believe that evil spirits can exploit flaws in our personality and behavior. Much like bacteria, they can lodge themselves into a wound and exacerbate it. If left unchecked, they can spread and facilitate the hosting of other hostile spirits. For it is written in Scripture:

> So humble yourselves before God. Resist the devil, and he will flee from you.
>
> —JAMES 4:7 (NLT)

My sin was not knowing God's Word. I wasn't resisting the devil; I was oblivious to him and his minions. The occult conditioning I'd undergone over the last few years gave demonic entities a wide-open door to operate through me. They were firmly entrenched. I was at war with invisible foes that I didn't even know were foes; I didn't know the rules of engagement or how to fight back. And this, my friends, is the greatest weapon in the arsenal used by the kingdom of darkness: our ignorance. It's why occult orders like Freemasonry insist on the slow-boil process. The longer someone is exposed to these evil forces in ignorance, the easier it is for those forces to dig in and have their way with the person.

Left unchecked, people start thinking the manifestations and ailments are normal parts of life. The kingdom of darkness is desperate to keep its members and its operations hidden. Demons are outnumbered and running out of time. They desperately want to keep people from knowing that God has put their entire kingdom beneath our feet. I was getting dangerously close to figuring these things out, so they hit me with everything they had until I crumbled.

I was an emotional train wreck. My mind was a tangled mess of pain and suffering, yet somehow, I gathered enough strength to call my sister Suzanne. I shouldn't have been able to do that, but I suspect that the Holy Spirit was helping me. I didn't know it yet, but salvation was at hand, in more ways than one.

As much as I tried to keep it together, I broke down, sobbing uncontrollably while speaking with Suzanne. There was no brave front for me to put up, and I suspected she knew I had hit rock bottom. She offered to drive the two-hour one-way trip to pick me up. Part of me wanted to accept, but the other part knew what a tremendous inconvenience it was for her. I told her that if I didn't feel better by morning, I'd take her up on her offer.

I didn't get much sleep that night, despite being utterly exhausted. During those hours I realized my emotional state was so dire that the slightest nudge or mishap could lead to something catastrophic and final. When Suzanne called back the next morning, I accepted her offer.

The drive to Suzanne's place was mostly quiet. I developed some pain and tightness in my right foot, something I'd never experienced before, so I was limping besides everything else. Maybe the fresh country air or just being out of the city would change my outlook on things, but no such luck. As I sat on Suzanne's back porch, looking out into the lush green trees, I felt no relief.

The look of utter despair on my face scared her almost as much as it scared me. The lamp had run dry, and not only did I not know what to do, I had no energy to do anything. She suggested a nap, so I curled up on her couch while she went to lie down on her bed.

I couldn't sleep, and all my problems felt larger than ever, so I closed my eyes. In my mind, I cried out, *I'm at the end of my rope, God; please show me the way!* And then it happened.

CHAPTER 21
THE IN BETWEEN

I struggle to explain the sensation of sheer peace that came over me and how gentle it was; like a morning fog dissipating in the rising sun. The thoughts of darkness and despair that had seemed so pervasive, so numerous, and overwhelming simply evaporated.

I saw my father as a young boy. A boy who was abused, had experienced poverty, starvation, and war, and had suffered, just as I had. A boy who became a man, normalized and integrated his abuse going forth, repeating it with his children. There was no more anger or hatred; those feelings had melted away, replaced with compassion. I also understood that I had lashed back at him in my pain, making a tense situation worse.

I no longer felt tired. Instead, I felt strangely refreshed and light. I bolted into an upright seating position, and Suzanne came to see what was going on. She looked like someone had slapped her, her expression a mixture of shock and wonder while staring at me. "Your face," she said, "it's completely changed!"

The only thing I could think to say was, "I understand now." She sat beside me, as I explained what I just experienced. I don't know how God did what He did, and truthfully, I don't need to. I cried out to Him, and He answered me. He saved me!

He shall call upon me, and I will answer him: I will be with him in trouble; I will deliver him, and honour him.

— PSALM 91:15 (KJV)

For whosoever shall call upon the name of the Lord shall be saved.

— ROMANS 10:13 (KJV)

I had been a rotten person, having turned away from God and worshipped idols. I had given demons free rein over my life and mind, made vile and wicked people my friends and willfully sinned and did witchcraft. I was a wrathful, lustful fornicator and a murderer who wasn't even fit to tie John the Baptist's sandals. But despite all that, God saved me! He had a plan, and He wasn't finished yet.

While He put out the raging fires in my life, I still had to do my part. This is how you know the Lord has touched you: the obstacles that once seemed insurmountable and overwhelming now feel like little speedbumps. All the problems before my salvation were still real, but I no longer dreaded the prospect of confronting them. In fact, I suddenly felt compelled to face them, and I knew He was with me. And now, I needed to do the one thing I thought I'd never do, I needed to forgive my dad.

The following evening, I hugged my sister, boarded a bus, and promptly returned to Montreal. The thought of doing what I intended once seemed impossible, but with God, all things are possible, and He wants us to succeed!

In his typical fashion, my dad was hard to find, always scurrying about and keeping himself busy. I went to my parents' house and waited for him. He eventually showed up. By his expression upon seeing me, I knew he was feeling remorseful for what had transpired days before. Taking him aside, I told him I was sorry for all the times I'd lashed out at him and that I knew he was suffering; I said that I didn't want him to suffer anymore, and that I forgave him. I took him in my arms and hugged him, and we both cried. I never felt so much compassion for my dad in my life. With tears running down his face, he told me he didn't want me to leave my apartment.

I undid What the kingdom of darkness had spent decades crafting and building in less than 48 hours. What I experienced was only the initial effects of God's miraculous healing. From this point forward, my life changed dramatically.

For one, I was no longer angry and bitter. I felt light, and while it was previously much easier to provoke me to anger, things seemed just to roll off my back now. The problems were the same, but I was different, and all those problems seemed trivial. What's more, whereas I had been prone to regular bouts of depression for as long as I can remember, those were also gone. I was now consistently happy and upbeat, and I remain so to this day.

My relationship with my dad improved. I was no longer annoyed by his mere presence, but actually enjoyed his company. In addition, my diet and eating habits changed. While I was once prone to binge-eating with a serious lust for sugar-laden foods, I was now foregoing all junk foods and integrating fasting into my life. As a result, I went from 240 lbs. down to about 190 lbs. in barely six months. Energy crashes were a thing of the past; I had stable energy throughout the day, and all cravings were gone.

I rekindled my passion for work and gradually got my business back up and running. During my downtime, I wrote everything I'd done wrong throughout my life and acknowledged responsibility for my failures. My finances were in bad shape, but that was OK. If poverty was my lot in life, I'd face it with dignity.

God must have been listening because He didn't let that go on for too long. Some relatively obscure investments that I'd made in the past, things that remained dormant and uncertain, suddenly bore fruit. Within a few months, my savings had been restored—with considerable interest. We truly serve a God of miracles!

Looking back on the situation, the best explanation for what happened to me on my sister's couch could be called an exorcism or deliverance. There's no way a person can undergo such a drastic change in such a short time, free of any side effects or bizarre reactions—without God. Not only was I changed in the moment, but to this day, all of those positive changes remain, and things continue to improve as I pray and immerse myself in the Word.

I eventually ran into Franco, Pierre, and several other Freemasons from my old life at a social event in August 2017. They were all the same, but I wasn't. There was no dread on my part; I felt free. Several of them even tried to talk me into returning to the Craft, claiming they needed "people like me," but I wasn't having any of it. What on earth could they possibly offer me? I was a new creature, set free from my past torments, from that ungodly order and the filthy list of historical degenerates they venerate. I had no reason to look back and every reason to look forward.

All the devil has to tempt us with is moldy leftovers; we settle for and praise leftovers as things to be admired and sought after while ignoring the banquet that the Lord has prepared for us. But so many people don't know this!

While the Lord had dealt the forces of darkness a commanding uppercut and sent them running for the hills, I wasn't out of the woods yet. Life was going well, but some things still needed to be dealt with. For one, I was still seeing those points of light. I occasionally had unwelcomed, invisible "visitors" who signaled their presence by either a lamp turning itself on or the sensation of someone on my bed when I'd be in a light sleep.

When turning the lights out at night, I saw these vague, dark shapes in my room and around my bed. If I closed my eyes for about 30 seconds to let them adapt to the darkness, I could open my eyes, relax my vision, and see them more clearly. I knew these were spirits, but I wasn't sure how to deal with them.

In a comedic way, it was as if some bully your dad beat up came to your window, meekly looking in, asking, "We good, bro?" We weren't good, not by a long shot! In fact, one day, as I was working at my computer desk, the lamp at the other end of the room, the one that had come on by itself so many times before, lit up. I was no longer curious but incensed at the phenomenon and barked in an unwelcoming tone, "You're not welcome here; get out!"

It took 3 or 4 tries of me telling that entity to take a hike, and one day, that lamp just stopped turning on by itself. I even checked to make sure the bulb and the outlet were all functional, which they were. Seems like *it* finally got the point.

While much of my sinful living was behind me, a few threads still needed to be trimmed. First, I wasn't praying or reading the

Bible yet. Second, I was still prone to using copious amounts of coarse language. Third, since I'd spent so much time researching on the internet, I had also allowed my eyes to wander and developed an addiction to pornography. These are a few of the other ways demons can get a foothold on our lives. It's not so much when we occasionally sin, but when we engage in sinful behaviors that become a lifestyle, it becomes a big problem. Promiscuity, lust, foul language, or simply not governing our thoughts, and doing such things regularly open us up to demonic activity. Not to mention consuming media that glorifies and/or promotes evil, ungodly behaviors. But just as before, God had a plan to kill several birds with one stone, and again, He used something that the enemy meant for evil, and He turned it for good.

CHAPTER 22
CONNECTING THE DOTS

In the late spring of 2018, I stumbled upon a horror movie called "Hereditary."[1] I hadn't watched anything truly scary in years and usually avoided such things. Still, something told me I needed to watch this one—God was about to scare me straight. I'll give you an overview, so you won't need to watch the movie: The plot revolves around a woman named Annie whose mother, Ellen, just died. As they go through her belongings, Annie and her husband discover she was part of a secret society. Annie and her mother were estranged for several years before her passing because of Ellen's controlling behavior and fascination with her two children.

One night, Annie's son, Peter, goes to a party and at his mother's insistence, takes his 13-year-old sister, Charlie, with him. At the party, Peter gets stoned, and Charlie unknowingly eats something she is allergic to and goes into anaphylactic shock. Peter frantically tries to drive her to the hospital. Charlie sticks her head out the window gasping for air, just as Peter swerves to avoid an animal on the road, and a utility pole decapitates Charlie.

Stricken with grief at the loss of her child, Annie is befriended by a woman named Joan, who is part of a "support group." One night, Joan gives Annie instructions on performing a seance to allow her to contact Charlie. Desperate, Annie convinces her family to perform the seance, during which she is seemingly possessed by Charlie until her husband douses her with water. Thinking she made a mistake, Annie throws Charlie's old sketchbook into the fireplace, and the sleeve of her sweater suddenly bursts into flames—until she retrieves the sketchbook, and the flames disappear. Annie seeks Joan out once again, only to discover that Joan has vanished.

During this time, Peter sees strange points of light, much like the ones I've seen. He sees the flashes of light one day at school, signaling the presence of an entity. Suddenly, Peter's head is propelled forward onto his desk, violently breaking his nose. Upon going through her mother's things, Annie discovers a book with information about a demon named Paimon, who seeks to inhabit the body of a young male. Annie's mother had used Charlie as Paimon's first fleshly vessel, but because of Charlie's mental deficiency, the demon wasn't able to fully manifest itself. Annie then discovers the decapitated body of a woman in the attic of her house, which she believes is her own mother's. After a series of gruesome events, Annie becomes possessed by the spirit of Paimon and decapitates herself with piano wire. Peter ends up falling out of a second-story window and dies. One of those specs of light enters Peter's corpse, and he revives, now possessed by the demon Paimon. All the events since Ellen's funeral had been orchestrated by the secret society. Paimon had been "trapped" in Charlie's body, so they needed to kill her to free him, then get Annie to perform a ritual to draw Paimon back; this time into the intended host, which was her son.

Leave it to the Lord to use the most unlikely tool as a lever to promote positive change in my life! Most of the horror movies I'd seen over the years relied on gore, suspense, and a great deal of exaggeration to generate fear in the viewer, but this movie was different. While some exaggeration existed, the ritual in the movie sent chills down my spine. I remembered the chants and various rituals we'd performed in the Lodge and the weekend workshops, seemingly benign at the time. Now, the nefarious aspect was revealed to me, as though God wanted me to see the true, hidden objectives of secret societies.

As images flashed across the screen, I began connecting the data points I'd accumulated over the years. I saw the correlation between New Age, Freemasonry, and every other order. They all lead back to that fallen would-be deity, who tried to exalt himself above the throne of the Most High God. The one who previously shone like the sun, who was so very close to God until he became corrupt and was cast into the abyss. The one named Lucifer, El, the Black Sun, Helios, Shemesh, Moloch, the Lord of the Rings, the fallen cherub whom Nimrod venerated and emulated in his rebellion against the Creator of the universe. This also explains the motto on the Great Seal of the United States, which reads, "E pluribus unum," Latin for, "Out of many, one." That's to say, many names, one god.

While many such movies are shameless vehicles for propaganda and dissemination of demonic influence, they offer astute viewers insight into the intentions of the kingdom of darkness. I don't think it's a stretch to believe that spiritual evil has been collaborating with wicked people, using occult rituals to allow unclean spirits to inhabit human bodies. While this may provide evil with physicality, at least for a time. Human bodies age, decay, and eventually fail. Therefore, the process needs to be repeated every few years, with varying degrees of success. An imperfect solution, to say the least.

In the last few decades, we've seen much emphasis placed on cybernetic enhancements, promises of having all our "smart" devices integrated into our bodies, and projected life spans of 200 years or more. This is just my opinion, but I don't think they intended this for the common person. We may simply be the guinea pigs used to beta-test the equipment. The true benefactors of technology will be the heavenly spirits who abandoned their first estate, rebelled against the one true God, and sought to make themselves the permanent, quasi-immortal rulers of this world.

All those puzzle pieces suddenly fit perfectly together, showing me the horror and perversity I had associated with and taken part in. I can't come close to describing the sorrow and shame I felt for what I'd been a part of and how much I'd grieved the Lord.

Despite it all, He still loved me and guided me back home. To this day, my mind has difficulty grasping the degree and depth of God's love and compassion for us. Perhaps we should all be baffled by it, for His love defies anything we can process in this fallen world. And because God so loved me, I made it my mission to share my bumpy, painful, and shameful journey with you, to share how God saved me from judgment and how He can do the same for you. He's knocking at the door of your heart right now; all you have to do is let Him in.

CHAPTER 23
MIRACLES, SIGNS AND WONDERS

THE MIRACLES

I am amazed at the Lord's means to get His message across to us. Just when I thought God had played His best hand in my life and miracles were done with, He surprised me yet again… and again!

For over two years, I immersed myself in at-home Bible studies, reading and re-reading, gleaning as much information as possible from the best Biblical scholars I could find. In the Fall of 2020, the Lord told me it was time to come out of isolation and find a church—so I did.

Unless you've been living inside an asteroid in deep space, you are painfully aware that it was about this time when the manufactured sickness—which shall remain nameless—was sweeping over the globe. Canada entered what I call "peak insanity." Despite all this, what God put in my heart was simply too important to ignore.

I scoured the internet for a Spirit-filled church, but most churches I'd found seemed lifeless, were unreasonably far away, or had shut down entirely. Except for one church. Because the Lord has a sense of humor, the most Spirit-filled and blessed church I've ever been to in my life was close enough for me to crawl there on my hands and knees. Well-played, Lord, well-played!

Fast-forward to early January 2021, and this church embarked upon 21 days of fasting and prayer. I was keeping an eye on my elderly mother, who had been released from the hospital barely a month earlier. Because of her fragile state, I volunteered to pick up groceries for her and my father to save them from unnecessary outings. On Monday, January 4th, my mom asked me to pick up a jar of peanut butter and presented me with a store coupon. I glanced down at it, trying to make out the brand name, and to my surprise, it said: *MaraNatha*!

For those of you not familiar with that term, it's Aramaic. Maranatha can mean "Our Lord comes, Our Lord is coming," or in the imperative, "Come, Lord!" At first, I thought this had to be a mistake in the flyer. But I ventured out in search of the artifact, anyway. It wasn't a mistake. Upon arriving in the right aisle, I met with a counter full of peanut butter jars with a bold "Mara-Natha" logo staring me right in the face...almost like the Lord was trying to tell me something.

I paid for the groceries and remembered I hadn't gotten a calendar for the new year. Most calendars are sold out by the time January rolls around, but he who doesn't seek, doesn't find, so off I went to the local pharmacy in search of one.

Upon asking the teller if they had any calendars left, she replied, "No, I don't think so," quickly followed by, "wait, let me check." She went behind the counter and disappeared into the back room for a moment. When she returned, she held a calendar with a beautifully painted portrait of Jesus on the cover. I gleefully accepted after promptly picking my jaw off the floor. Upon inquiring about the item's price, she told me it was *free*. She tried slipping the calendar through the slot at the bottom of the plexiglass divider, but it wouldn't fit, so she had to pass it to me over the top of the panel—*Jesus overcomes!*

About two days before, I was at home praying and wondering if God really heard our prayers. These two "signs" occurred barely an hour apart on the same day, and the symbolism of what was happening wasn't lost on me.

Over the next few months, the church of Jesus Christ would see itself tested as never before in Canada. Despite some genuinely frightening moments with Pastors being unlawfully harassed, arrested, imprisoned, churches being forced to close, and some literally being burned to the ground, our church came through it all, slightly shaken but unscathed. It's as though the Lord was letting me know things were going to be OK, that He was with us and watching over us, that our prayers were being heard—and answered.

THE HEALINGS

About a year later, in the early days of the annual 21-day period of fasting and prayer, I experienced strange pains in my lower abdomen. These pains came several months earlier. The discomfort not only disrupted my sleep, but I started needing to use the bathroom in the middle of the night, which was foreign to me. Clearly, something wasn't right, and it wasn't going away.

While a worldly person might feel compelled to seek a doctor, run a bunch of tests, take meds, and accept a "bad report" about managing this new condition, I wanted no part of it. Part of me suspected that the kingdom of darkness was looking for a weakness in my defenses and throwing things at me, hoping that something, anything, would stick.

On the third night of the fast, the pain struck again. It was 1:30 a.m., and I could not sleep, restlessly tossing and turning as my lower abdomen felt like it was being squeezed from the inside. And then I realized hey, dummy, you have the Holy Spirit, the same Spirit that raised Jesus from the dead now *lives in you!*

It's fascinating how we can read the Holy Scriptures repeatedly and gloss over some of the most significant passages. Such passages hold the keys to our transformation. With this newfound understanding, I simply stated in a calm, confident voice, "In Jesus' name, I *am* healed!" And that's when it happened. Within fifteen to twenty seconds, the pain subsided—completely! I was so utterly overjoyed that I was wide awake from the sheer excitement of the miracle I'd just experienced. At that very moment, I understood the power of faith and its critical role in our ability to perform and receive miracles from the Lord.

> *"Truly I tell you, if anyone says to this mountain, 'Go, throw yourself into the sea,' and does not doubt in their heart but believes that what they say will happen, it will be done for them."*
>
> — MARK 11:23 (NIV)

The nighttime bathroom excursions stopped, and while the pain tried to creep in one more time about a month later, I merely repeated my proclamation. It went away and hasn't returned since.

> *"If you listen carefully to the Lord your God and do what is right in his eyes, if you pay attention to his commands and keep all his*

> *decrees, I will not bring on you any of the diseases I brought on the Egyptians, for I am the Lord, who heals you."*

> — EXODUS 15:26 (NIV)

On one Sunday service at our church, a sister in Christ arrived with a tense look on her face. She hadn't been feeling well since the Friday prior. She was experiencing unwelcome gastrointestinal distress and a marked loss of appetite. It was so bad that she contemplated skipping church altogether and running back home. Before the service, her husband and I laid hands on her and prayed for healing. And after the service, she felt better! When I saw her later that evening, her appetite had returned, and she was on the mend. In fact, during that Sunday evening service, there was an unexpected breakout of testimonies from people of all ages relating to various miraculous events.

GOD TRANSFORMS

Perhaps the most unusual of these miracles is the one I wear on my wrist. Almost fifteen years ago, I spoiled myself with a brand-new mechanical luxury watch. While its functionality was precarious from the start, it stopped working entirely about five years ago. After prying open the case, I discovered the culprit—rust on the watch movement. The gasket was compromised, and water had seeped in and corroded the mechanism. Since I was already in financial straits, and the cost of repairing it was high, I placed it back in its box, burying it in my closet. It remained there until I had the sudden urge to revisit it.

This watch was severely damaged and would *not* be functional without extensive watch-making surgery. It had impossibly small gears that were corroded, and the springs were rusted. If you've ever dealt with a rusty screw or pipe in your house, you know how corrosion seizes parts, so you can imagine how much more problematic it is with tiny, intricate pieces. The special oils that lubricate those delicate moving parts get soaked up by the rust, and everything just grinds to a halt. At that point, the only thing to do is replace the parts or the entire movement. I tried to get it running several times before storing it, but nothing could be done—or so I thought.

Now that I was in a much better financial situation, I could've simply sent the watch to the service center for repairs, but I had a better idea. Why give money to the watch company when I could donate it to the church and advance God's Kingdom? So that's exactly what I did. I prayed to God and thanked Him for hearing and answering my prayers. I sowed a financial seed equivalent to the cost of the repairs, expecting my Heavenly Father would restore the watch. I sealed the donation envelope, picked up the watch, and began gently shaking it to wind it. It worked!

I was beside myself, staring at the second hand ticking-away as if the watch had never stopped. I thought to myself, "This is impossible; I saw the rust with my own eyes." I knew there was no physical way for it to work, yet it did! Unable to contain my curiosity, I pulled out my tools and unscrewed the case back, determined to see what was happening inside this watch. Upon removing it and peering inside, my expression must have been priceless: there wasn't a trace of rust anywhere! The movement looked brand new, and it just kept on ticking. As of writing this, the watch continues to work, and while it runs a tad slow, it remains miraculously functional.

Truly, we serve a God of miracles.

Upon seeing the watch's movement entirely changed, it reminded me of how God had transformed Moses' staff into a serpent in the Book of Exodus. God took an everyday object and caused it to change into something completely different.

> *Then the Lord asked him, "What is that in your hand?"*
> *"A staff," he replied.*
> *The Lord said, "Throw it on the ground."*
> *Moses threw it on the ground and it became a snake, and he ran*
> *from it. Then the Lord said to him, "Reach out your hand and*
> *take it by the tail."*
> *So Moses reached out and took hold of the snake and it turned back*
> *into a staff in his hand.*
>
> — EXODUS 4:2-4 (NIV)

We truly serve the God of miracles

CHAPTER 24
SOBERING THOUGHTS

The God we serve is all-powerful, all-knowing, wise, and compassionate beyond measure. He truly is the God of miracles, yet we should not mistakenly assume that when we accept Jesus into our hearts, all of life's troubles suddenly disappear or that our lives will be obstacle-free. If you look at the Apostles, who, after deciding to follow Jesus, lived Spirit-filled lives and performed many miracles, yet their lives were far from easy. In fact, history shows us that all the Apostles died as martyrs, other than John, who died of old age, but not before the Roman Emperor Domitian attempted to have him boiled to death in oil.

Countless are the martyrs who were maligned, persecuted, tortured, and murdered for their faith in Jesus Christ over the last two thousand years. That persecution continues to this day and will follow believers to the very end, as the Book of Revelation clearly states.

While many who suffer are compelled to turn to Jesus, and rightly so, your life may be very happy. You may have never known financial hardship, or a troubled childhood. Maybe your children are happy and well-adjusted. Perhaps you live in a wonderful home, and you love your job. If asked, you might even say that you're a pretty good person—a citizen of exemplary behavior, a model of virtue for neighbors and co-workers alike. Why would you want to take up your cross and follow Jesus?

Just for fun, tell me:

- Have you ever told a lie? Even just a little white lie?
- Have you ever had lustful thoughts about someone who wasn't your spouse?
- Have you ever idolized a celebrity?
- Have you ever stolen something?
- Have you ever misused God's name?
- Have you ever worked on a Sunday?
- Have you ever failed to honor your parents?
- Have you ever been obsessed with a sport, a car, or a new electronic device?
- Have you ever hated someone?
- Have you ever wanted something someone else had so badly that you thought about taking it from them?

If you answered yes to just one of these questions, congratulations, you've sinned! You've most likely broken every single one of God's commandments repeatedly. While you might be perfectly righteous in your own sight, you will not be your own judge; God will. If it's any consolation, you're not alone. The Bible tells us:

For all have sinned and fall short of the glory of God.

— ROMANS 3:23 (NIV)

In case you aren't sure what the text means by "all," it means everyone; you, me, that guy in the baseball cap across the street—everyone. And if you ask what the penalty for sin is? Once again, the Bible has the answer. Brace yourself, for it says:

For the wages of sin is death, [...].

— ROMANS 6:23 (NIV)

In fact, let's read what the Book of Revelation tells us will happen to sinners:

Then I saw a great white throne and him who was seated on it. The earth and the heavens fled from his presence, and there was no place for them. And I saw the dead, great and small, standing before the throne, and books were opened. Another book was opened, which is the book of life. The dead were judged according to what they had done as recorded in the books. The sea gave up the dead that were in it, and death and Hades gave up the dead that were in them, and each person was judged according to what they had done. Then death and Hades were thrown into the lake of fire. The lake of fire is the second death. Anyone whose name was not found written in the book of life was thrown into the lake of fire.

— REVELATION 20: 11-15 (NIV)

But the cowardly, the unbelieving, the vile, the murderers, the sexually immoral, those who practice magic arts, the idolaters and all liars—they will be consigned to the fiery lake of burning sulfur. This is the second death.

— REVELATION 21: 8 (NIV)

It's a sobering and unpleasant outcome for sinners, is it not? And yet that's what every sinner deserves. You might be living high on the hog right now, but the grave and judgement await everyone.

> *What good is it for someone to gain the whole world, yet forfeit their soul?*

> — MARK 8:36 (NIV)

The worst part is that you haven't gained the whole world, not even close! In fact, as a sinner, if you take a step back and evaluate your life, you're dooming yourself to eternal hellfire for mere crumbs.

What if I told you that while you clearly deserved the death penalty, someone came along and paid your debt just as you were on your way to receiving your sentence. How would you feel? I'm pretty sure you'd be humbled and deeply touched by that person's act of generosity. I'm sure you'd feel indebted to that person for what they did. They didn't do it because you're worthy; you're not. None of us are. They paid your debt because they love you!

That's what Jesus did on the cross, which is why *you need Jesus*. We all do! God is perfect in all His ways, and because He loves you, He sent His only son to come and pay your debt and free you from the chains of sin and death. All you have to do is:

- Admit that you're a sinner;
- believe in your heart that Jesus is the Son of God;
- repent of your sins;
- confess with your mouth that Jesus Christ is Lord;
- make a decision to be baptized in water and live a holy life.

The Mosaic Law is perfect, but we aren't, and God knows that. The Law was a mirror for us, something we could hold up to see ourselves as we really are and know just how impossible it is for us to be righteous of our own doing. The Law intended to show man just how much he needs God. This is why Jesus said:

"Be perfect, therefore, as your heavenly Father is perfect."

— MATTHEW 5:48 (NIV)

What Jesus said in the previous verse, stunned His audience. He said it to get them to understand that despite their outward appearance of righteousness, there was no way for them to meet that standard of perfection by themselves. So God made a way for us through His Son, Jesus.

CHAPTER 25

Think of your body and your life like a car: they come in all sizes, shapes, and colors. God's Word is like your GPS, guiding you throughout your life's journey. God intended our fleshly vessels to be perfect. Adam and Eve brought sin into the equation, leading to "manufacturing defects" on the production line. This means that some vessels come off the line with problems from the start, and others don't have issues and are properly used and taken care of, yet all will eventually still break down and fail.

Add in all the questionable things we do throughout our lives: eat poorly, consume excessive alcohol, fail to exercise, etc. Those things put extra wear on the vessel. Many also stray from our GPS's guidance and end up off-road or stuck in ditches.

Sometimes the car isn't perfect, but it works well enough. Despite that, we try our luck, running recklessly through an intersection or two. Most times, we're lucky, and nothing bad happens. But if you run those yellow lights often enough, you'll eventually collide with an immovable object. Sometimes we end up standing at the corner of an intersection, dazed and confused, holding nothing but a broken hub cap and the steering wheel because that's all that's left of our car after we utterly totaled it.

Shattered and filled with despair, we speak with a colleague who tells us about this marvelous mechanic they know named Jesus. They tell us that Jesus is a specialist at rebuilding wrecks. Not thoroughly convinced but desperate, we seek out this Jesus guy. We show up at His garage, dragging the shattered remains with us. He tells us that everything will be OK, we can just leave our car there, and He'll have it fixed by 4 p.m. tomorrow.

Car? What car? All I've got left is a busted hub cap and the steering wheel. The car's gone; what's left to fix!? Jesus politely assures us that He's used to this sort of thing but that this might be a particularly complex job, so make it 4:15 p.m. instead.

Frustrated and filled with disbelief, we grudgingly do as we're told, convinced the situation is hopeless. We walk back to the garage the next day, expecting to be told that nothing can be done or that it'll be months before we can expect any results. Upon walking in, we're surprised to see a car that looks eerily like our destroyed car, except it looks new! Same color, same upholstery, and same option package, but it can't be. The formerly squeaky door handle makes no noise, it feels brand new! We check the serial number on the dash—it's *our* car!

We hesitantly walk up to Jesus and ask, "Is. is this my car?" And Jesus nods while inspecting the paperwork. Amazed, we stammer, "But how can this even be? There was nothing left. This is impossible!!" Jesus lifts His eyes to us and calmly says, "For you, some things are impossible, but not for Me."

Now we're getting nervous because we realize this was a colossal job. At this point we realize we may not even be able to afford the work. So, we nervously ask, "What do I owe you?" and Jesus, still leafing through His work orders, calmly looks at us and says, "It's already paid for. Now go and sin no more."

That's Jesus! When you think you've utterly destroyed your life beyond hope of any recovery, He can fix it. He already paid your unpayable tab because He loves you. All He asks is that we believe He is who Scripture says He is and that we repent of our sins. We get an eternity of bliss in His presence for this meager price. What belief system, organization, or religion can possibly compare with that?

How many miracles are attributed to Buddha, Mohammed, or Brahma? How many people have been healed by these prophets/gods? How many people have been raised from the dead? How many demons have been cast out in the name of these so-called deities?

It's true, as Christians, we must forego some pleasures and the vices this life offers, but is that truly the burden we believe it to be? Are all or any of these temporal "pleasures" really worth spending an eternity in the lake of fire for? Carefully scrutinize the lives of this world's secular idols, whether athletes, movie stars, business magnates, or others. They have money, power, prestige, and all the delights of the flesh, yet how many are truly happy? And even if they claim to be happy now, how will that fleeting happiness measure against the torment they will suffer in the afterlife? They might bribe earthly police, judges, and politicians, but they can't take it with them when they die, nor can those riches be used to bribe God.

Despite all the things I've given up for the love of Christ, I can tell you with no hesitation that I'm far, far happier, and healthier than ever. While many people have been thrown out of work and/or their homes over the alleged crisis created by that unnamed illness, driven to depression, despair, alcoholism, conjugal violence, drug abuse, and suicide, my situation has been largely unaffected by the political and economic turmoil. In fact, my life has gotten better. Events that would certainly have wrecked the version of me-from-five-years-ago now roll off my back effortlessly.

There are still challenges and difficult situations, but they all seem much smaller and unimportant now. The more I pray and give my issues over to God, the more peaceful my life becomes. Better still, I have the promise that I'll have a far more glorious existence in the next life than I could ever hope to have in this one, free of death, disease, heartache, cruelty, and injustice. Can you confidently say the same?

AFTERWORD

Take a moment and ask yourself this simple question: do you know where you're going once you die?

Many people are trapped in the New Age belief system and the occult; you may be one of them. If so, I implore you to ponder what I've written in this book. I urge you to test the foundations of what you think you know and see how well it holds up to the Gospel. There's too much at stake to put it off. Eternity is a very long time to spend regretting making the wrong decision. God wants something better for you, and so do I.

> *For whosoever shall call upon the name of the Lord shall be saved.*

> — ROMANS 10:13 (KJV)

SALVATION PRAYER

Don't let another second of your life pass. Pray this prayer today to start your brand new life as a child of the most-high God!

Dear Heavenly Father, I surrender my life to You. I declare that Satan's power over me is forever broken; he is a defeated foe who is trampled beneath my feet, and his kingdom will fall. Because of the blood of Jesus, I am no longer a slave to sin. Because of Your promises, I proceed not toward victory but from victory!
I declare with joy that Jesus Christ is my Lord and Savior; He died on the cross for our sins and was resurrected to everlasting glory after three days! Thank You, Heavenly Father, for as a child of God, I have been washed clean by the blood of the lamb and was made righteous in Your sight.
I receive by faith all the promises, abundance, and healing that You intend for my life and reaffirm my allegiance to Christ Jesus, the Son of God.
Heavenly Father, thank You for making me the head and not the tail; thank You that I am seated with Jesus in heavenly places and crowned with glory. I receive it and call it done in Jesus' name, amen!

ACKNOWLEDGMENT

This book would never have been possible without the help and research of Dr. Michael S. Heiser. Though we sadly never met, and will never meet this side of heaven, Dr. Heiser was the academic giant upon whose shoulders this work was made possible. His research has not only inspired numerous other biblical scholars, but I can safely say that the head-start his research provided shaved a decade off my own studies and allowed this book to leap forward several years in time. My first exposure to Dr. Heiser's work was through a fictional novel of his entitled The Facade, which I discovered in early 2007. Upon opening the book on that fateful Winter's day, a seed was planted and continues to grow. Despite being a scholar of the highest order, he was gifted with the ability to make difficult and obscure subjects understandable, and the ability to do so with a degree of humility we should all strive for.

Though he has gone to his reward, Dr. Heiser's body of work remains, and continues to shed light on those strange passages of the Bible few people outside academic circles have dared to tackle.

Mike, I'm firmly convinced that I was led to your work by the Holy Spirit, and I can't thank you enough for everything you've done to help propel our understanding of the Bible forward!

Notes

CHAPTER 1

1. *The Ten Commandments*, directed by Cecil B. DeMille (Los Angeles, CA: Paramount Pictures, 1956) Blu-ray.

CHAPTER 6

1. *Occult Forces*, directed by Jean Mamy (Vichy, France: Nova Films, 1943). Digital file.

CHAPTER 8

1. Derek Prince, *They Shall Expel Demons* (Ada, MI: Chosen Books, 1998).

CHAPTER 15

1. *Transformers: Revenge of the Fallen*, directed by Michael Bay (Los Angeles, CA: Paramount Pictures, 2009). Blu-Ray.
2. https://www.yahwehswordarchives.org/book_of_jubilees/index.htm
3. https://biblehub.com/commentaries/genesis/10-9.htm

CHAPTER 22

1. *Hereditary*, directed by Ari Aster, Los Angeles, CA: PalmStar Media (2018). Digital file.

ABOUT THE AUTHOR

John F. Moscato is a Canadian-born product designer and stylist who began his career as a freelance illustrator and designer for Janus Publications/Dream Pod 9 in the early 90s. While still a student at Dawson College, John was noticed by a talent scout for his unusual creative abilities and illustration skills. He made his first splash on the role-playing game scene as the  mechanical designer and illustrator for the "Jovian Chronicles" sourcebook, as well as the RPG-turned-video-game series "Heavy Gear."

Unsatisfied by the limitations of an illustrator's career path, John was driven to learn the art of pattern-making and product design, turning his and his client's many product ideas into reality: a career path he pursues to this day.

You can email John Moscato through his publisher:

info@RiseUpPublications.com